We Are One

Muriel Gladney

When the enemy threatens your destiny,
activate your built-in I.P.S. system

BookLocker

Copyright © 2019 Muriel Gladney

Paperback ISBN: 978-1-64438-719-1
Hardcover ISBN: 978-1-64438-720-7

All rights reserved. No part of this publication may be reproduced, stored in a retrieval system, or transmitted in any form or by any means, electronic, mechanical, recording or otherwise, without the prior written permission of the author.

Published by BookLocker.com, Inc., St. Petersburg, Florida.

Printed on acid-free paper.

BookLocker.com, Inc.
2019

First Edition

Scripture taken from the New King James Version, Copyright © 1979, 1980, 1982 by Thomas Nelson, Inc. Used by permission. All rights reserved. Scripture taken from the King James Version of the Bible. Revised Standard Version of the Bible, copyright © 1952 [2nd edition, 1971] by the Division of Christian Education of the National Council of the Churches of Christ in the United States of America. Used by permission. All rights reserved. New Revised Standard Version Bible, copyright © 1989, Division of Christian Education of the National Council of the Churches of Christ in the United States of America. Used by permission. All rights reserved.

Graphic Cover design provided by Otis Smith, www.Otitographics.com

Library of Congress Cataloging in Publication Data
Gladney, Muriel
We Are One by Muriel Gladney
RELIGION / Christian Living / General | RELIGION / Christian Living / Calling & Vocation| RELIGION / Christian Living / Family & Relationships
Library of Congress Control Number: 2019904352

Dedication Page

First and foremost, this book is a tribute to and a thank you to Yahovah, our God and heavenly Father, and His Son, Jesus Christ, our Lord and Savior, for His guidance through His Holy Spirit.

I thank my daughter, Paige Centers, my son Thaddeus C. Centers, my friend and sister in Christ Gwendolyn Madison, and Farrell Chiles, [my friend and God-given brother], author of African American Warrant Officers: Preserving Their Legacy, for their steadfast support, encouragement, and inspiration, as I prepared this book as a testimony to God, His Son Jesus, and His Holy Spirit of the greatest gift of love the world will ever know.

Table of Contents

Introduction: God's Purposed Helper

History reveals that men alter the landscape of the world through war. According to the Word of God, women are also appointed to change the world, but in a different manner. Given the historical chronicles of the *same* unceasing acts of cruelty against women, the question must be asked.

Why are women—in particular—on Satan's hit list? It is an endless query. For the first time, this question is answered in *We Are One*.

God warned us in the beginning that we have an enemy. The stories in *We Are One* demonstrate that the devil is completely impartial in reaching his goal, regardless of race, religion, age, or nationality. The only difference is the location.

We Are One reveals a thought-provoking, yet life-altering biblical fact.

It *is* all about YOU, the woman, and your God-ordained mission.

In every instance of creation, God first spoke its specific design and purpose before its formation. Our world today proves His spoken Word is Eternal because *everything* still functions exactly as He said. Thus, when God *said* He made the woman to be a help-meet, i.e. a helper, the woman was *and is* imbued with the power and thus the ability to accomplish her divine *spoken* assignment.

But, it is *not* what women have been taught for centuries.

What is it? God knows. Satan knows. It is time for women to know. *We Are One* will divulge this amazing truth.

Satan initiated his goal in the Garden of Eden to deflect Eve from this God-ordained assignment. Yes, Eve *was* the devil's original target. Why? The importance of the woman's *true* and *unchanged* role up to today is the reason. This specific, life-altering task was given *only* to the woman. *We Are One* explains.

God's Declaration—for YOU, the woman—cannot be annulled.

The fulfillment of our divine appointed mission *will* change the world, as God intended. Therefore, He gave us everything we will ever need to complete our commission. In short, it involves activating our *in-built* I.P.S. system. It is a fail-safe guidance procedure that ensures the accomplishment of our task.

We Are One presents the impeccable brilliance of God's plan through several personal stories that show that our built-in I.P.S. system is eternal, and indestructible. These stories illustrate that during the passage of time, from the beginning of mankind to today, Satan is unchanged from his goal—to steal, kill, or destroy, the woman. Nevertheless, the testimonies of these women are a witness to Jesus that *nothing* can nullify what God has set in order.

In contrast, a few tales are included to illustrate the devastation that occurs in the lives of women who never discovered true wisdom as to the *why me* persecution in their lives. *We Are One* answers this question.

Women have been taught for centuries that bad things happen to us simply because we are female. And, or, we are the weaker sex, according to many in the religious arena.

We Are One illustrates that both concepts are *biblically* incorrect. God did *not* make no junk, nor a bargain basement creation when He special made the woman.

Eve made the mistake of trying to *help* the enemy before she was sufficiently saturated with the full strength of her I.P.S. system. Ladies, it is time to stop falling. Come and *see* why our I.P.S. system is essential in our Faith walk.

Every worldly enterprise insists that training is necessary. We go to college to *train* our brains until they are finely tuned. Athletes already have muscles in their bodies. However, no matter how talented they are, *training* builds and fine tunes their muscles.

Our I.P.S. system is like a muscle. It is *already instilled in* us by God. *We Are One* shows how training builds this *spiritual* muscle. When fully trained, you will be able to withstand the devil and stand.

Ladies, it is time to *Stand Up* like the lady in this first story. Why? The world is waiting for the *Sons of God* to arise.

That includes YOU.

Chapter 1 – A Petite Giant Killer

We can do all things through Him [Jesus,]
who strengthens me, Philippians 4: 15

T he children of Israel were dealing with a flesh and blood enemy Goliath whose size alone struck fear into the hearts of experienced adult warriors, *1 Samuel 17*. The men turned and fled in fear. King David, yet a youth at that time, heard the boasting of the enemy. His faith in God led him to ask the men around him what gifts would he receive if he slew the giant. The men mocked and taunted David, including his own family. When Goliath saw David, he also scorned him because of his youth and size.

However, it is written that David knew and trusted Yahovah, our heavenly father and God. Goliath told David *come on* so I can kill you. David said *I'm coming but I am coming in the name of the Lord* whom you have insulted. David ran towards the enemy and killed him with a stone.

It wasn't the stone. It was David's faith in God that gave him the victory.

Pilar Garcia's story is reminiscent of a current day David fighting Goliath. Standing a mere 4' 11", her battle against death, her *spiritual* Goliath, has spanned five decades.

Born in Ecuador, Pilar is now 72.

Pilar wanted to be a nun when she was young. She always believed in God because her aunts and uncles were the first missionaries in Ecuador. They often took her with them on their missions. However, her life would run a different course.

At the age of 22, she was on the plane that was kidnapped and taken to Cuba.

"Money was required by the government to be paid before the planes would be released," Pilar stated. "An additional price was charged for American citizens."

However, during the initial flight, she sensed something was wrong when she looked out of the window. She knew from previous trips they should have been flying over the mountains to their next destination to catch another plane to the United States. Instead they were flying over the ocean. She asked the stewardess what was going on. She admitted that they had been hijacked. Then, without warning, the man sitting next to Pilar pulled out a gun. He was one of the hijackers. Over the past few years, Pilar said she had heard that some of the hijackers are now living in the United States.

"I tried to find them on Facebook," Pilar said. "I couldn't locate them."

At the time of the hijacking, Pilar was living in the United States, but she often went back to Ecuador for vacation. When the plane landed in Cuba, they were not allowed to leave the airport. She was not yet married. However, she was ready to fight for her freedom.

A devout Catholic from childhood she knew God would protect her. She was 22 at the time. Some of the younger girls, ages 17 to 18, looked to her for strength. They were in Cuba for almost a week. During that time, they did not have a change of clothes. Pilar showed them how to wash their clothes and especially their underwear in the bathroom. One night they heard a strange sound. It was Pilar who opened the door to confront the possible attacker.

She returned home to the United States.

Death tried to sneak up on Pilar again. Although it was her first pregnancy, she kept trying to tell the doctor that something was wrong in her stomach. They insisted that she was simply homesick. She staunchly maintained her position and kept telling them that was not the problem. Her complaint was ignored. The baby was born in March of 1971. However, the pain in her stomach continued for another three months.

"At times it was so bad I felt like I was dying," Pilar stated.

Her husband kept insisting that she needed to go to Ecuador to see a doctor. She prepared to leave but she was so sick that she felt she was not going to make it. Then out of the blue, one of the doctors called her and asked her to come to the hospital right away.

"I was in so much pain that the mere touch of the sheets over my body hurt," Pilar said.

They took her to surgery and opened her up. But then told her that there was nothing they could do. In their opinion, she was going to die after they informed her what was wrong with her stomach.

Her stomach was full of pus. They could not even decide what to do because of the extent of the infection. The doctors gave her 24 hours to live. Pilar said about 40 doctors from teaching colleges came to see her and study her body because they could not figure out why she was still alive. They admitted that they had never seen this type of infection. They said it was a form of gangrene and had spread throughout her entire body. They hooked her up to tubes to drain the infection. Ten 5-gallon bottles later, they still could not figure out what it was or what had caused this type of infection. Pilar said it was the color of yellow egg yolks. She was in the hospital for three months because her gallbladder had also become infected. Every day, for about three months, the doctors would come into her hospital room and tell her that she had perhaps one more day to live.

"I prayed continually and asked God to heal me because I had a new daughter to raise," Pilar calmly stated.

In other words, she did not pray just for herself so she could just live. She knew the importance of raising her daughter. My ears have heard many testimonies from women over the years. And many are yet so traumatized by the past, they can barely talk. Pilar's Faith in God was so deep that she might as well have been talking about a kitchen recipe.

A second surgery was performed. The infection was still in her body but not as bad. The tubes, that had been draining the infection, had been in her for such an extended length of time that it hurt to pull them out.

Pilar was told not to have any more children. It was the doctor's consensus that it was the pregnancy that had caused the infection. Two years later she became pregnant again. The doctors insisted that she have an abortion.

Like David, Pilar stood her ground. She said no. She knew it was a miracle that she was even pregnant. Therefore, she was going to have this baby. It was a costly decision. She broke out in hives all over her entire body.

"I looked like a monster," Pilar stated.

When it was time for the baby's birth, she started bleeding extensively.

"I could hear the doctors saying that I was going to die," she said. "In my mind, I said no, I will not die. I kept praying that God would allow me to live because I had two children now to take care of."

God heard. She lived. The doctors told her husband to have a vasectomy.

Pilar and her husband had met and married in the United States. He was also from Ecuador. After the second child was born, he had started working for Dole pineapple Company. After getting his bachelor's degree, they moved back to Ecuador.

Life was normal for about 15 years. During this time, they had established a relationship with a friend who was a doctor. Pilar and her husband were godparents to his children. Suddenly one morning Pilar woke up with a feeling as though something sharp was in her throat.

She thought it was her tonsils. This doctor took her complaint serious and sent her to a cancer doctor. The diagnosis came back. She was in the last stages of throat cancer. And it was in the glands in her throat. They did a biopsy. Rather than rely on anyone, Pilar said she went to the pathologist to get her own report.

"I lied to get it," Pilar said. "I wanted to know for myself.

She asked the doctor how long she had to live. He stated three weeks. She said what about surgery. The surgeon told her there was no hope. *Pilar, the petite Giant Killer,* did not take no for an answer. After informing the surgeon that God was her hope and the Lord has the last word, she insisted on having the surgery.

She called a couple of members of her family, of whom one is a deacon, to tell the family to be at her mother's home that evening. The family came. Pilar called her dining room table the roundtable for family conversations.

She still does this at her home in the senior community in which she lives. Sometimes it is just girl talk. Sometimes it is for bible study groups.

Pilar told the family about the throat cancer. Her pituitary gland was also infected. Stranger still, the doctors said the cancer had started in her ovaries but spread to her throat.

Initially, the family wanted her husband to send her back to the United States. Pilar said no. The doctors had informed her that she needed a period of rest or she would bleed to death during the surgery. She also told her family that the country did not matter.

She explained to the family that if the Lord wanted her to be alive it would be so.

The petite but gentle Giant Killer stood firm.

Unlike King David's brothers, her family did not mock her. They finally understood because she had raised them to know God. They accepted her explanation. They prayed.

Talking to God was not strange to the family because both Pilar and her husband utilized prayer in every situation whether it was thanking God, or asking for help.

Privately, Pilar said she prayed to the Lord for a message.

"I am going to open my bible," she said she told God. "Please show me, give me a sign because I still have daughters to raise."

He answered.

She opened her Bible. It was the book of Isaiah, chapter 38, where Hezekiah was sick and about to die. God had heard his plea and extended his life for 15 more years. However, there was something more that God had the prophet tell Hezekiah.

Pilar picked up on this divine direction and utilized it to heal her body thousands of years after this biblical miracle with Hezekiah. In other words, God is unchanged in his love and care for those who trust him and believe in him.

Hezekiah's illness was due to boils. And the prophet Isaiah had told him to make a plaster of figs and lay them on the boils.

Pilar followed suit. The next day after reading the Scripture she went to the Farmer's market. However, figs were not in season. And in Ecuador, figs are usually used for Passover.

When we commit our lives to God in true love, He will give us the desires of our hearts,

Psalms 37: 4-5

Nevertheless, God was in control. A lady whom she knew from years before called out to her that she had figs. The next step was to prepare them.

People were available who would

prepare them for her. But, Pilar wanted to do it herself because it was God's message specifically to her. She boiled the figs until they were soft like smashed potatoes.

Remember, the cancer had started in her ovaries.

"I laid the plaster on my stomach that morning and left it on all day," Pilar said. "Then, I waited until my period came."

After getting ready for the surgery, her friend the doctor said do not let them do a biopsy on the tumors on her ovaries and the glands. At first the surgeon refused to operate. Then for some reason, he came back to Pilar and said that he didn't know why, but he would do the surgery. She also let him do the biopsy.

"Afterwards, I felt that literally I had a pain in my soul, just as her friend Otto had said," Pilar said. "I started crying. I didn't know what to think."

But God was still in control.

The surgeon who would perform her operation always prayed prior to surgery, and for his patients before operating. After the surgery was completed, the doctor told her there was literally a line inside of her body, almost as though it had been drawn with a pencil. The surgeon told Pilar that he took everything out below the line, including her fallopian tubes, her uterus, and ovaries. After the surgery, all lab tests showed that she no longer needed chemo for cancer. The cancer was gone.

Pilar recovered and raised her daughters.

Pilar returned to the United States. However, she started feeling bad in her stomach area again. The doctors had told her there was nothing wrong. Their diagnosis for her illness was that she was emotionally suffering from the loss of her husband. She flew back to Ecuador.

"Again, I felt so sick," she said. "It felt like I was going to die, again."

The doctors did a complete checkup. Her blood pressure was okay. Her sugar levels were okay. They didn't give up. They decided that an endoscopy was needed to find the source of her pain. She stayed at her brother's house. He was the only sibling still alive in Ecuador.

The procedure was recorded. The rest of the family was in a viewing room and could see what was happening.

The doctors discovered twenty polyps in her stomach. The recording showed that when the doctor opened up her stomach, the nurse made a face from the stench of the infection. The year was 2012. The doctors could not understand how she had been able to get on a plane and fly to Ecuador. The pressure alone could have caused the polyps to explode. They said it was a miracle that she survived.

Pilar, *the petite giant killer,* had no problem in telling them how she survived. She emphatically stated that it was the Lord who had kept her. Once she was back in the United States, Pilar tried to show the recording of the procedure to her American doctors. They refused to even look at it.

She stayed in Ecuador for three weeks. They gave her medication for six months because they knew the same medication was not available in the United States. She revisited Ecuador in 2014.

During these times that her life was in jeopardy, her faith never wavered. When asked did she ever wonder why she had to endure so much, and did her family's faith grow, Pilar responded as follows.

"I have believed since childhood that God loved me," Pilar stated. "They [the family] *watched* my faith hold steadfast no matter what the situation was. Now as adults, they tell me my faith taught them to do the same. However, if I were allowed to ask God one question, it would be this. Why do people who are mean and selfish seem to have a life void of pain."

I understand her question. But, one thing that I can declare as one who grew up without the benefit of instruction by a true godly family. Her family's dedication to teaching her about God when she was a child made the difference in her trust in God.

Now 72, Pilar is still going strong despite the enemy's attempt to take her out. More so, her I.P.S. system simply got stronger with each attack.

The knowledge of God is the fertilizer for the I.P.S. system that is within every woman. For those who do not receive this nourishment at an early age, the journey to complete reliance upon the I.P.S. system is more perilous. In fact, sometimes it takes another Damascus Fall to make God's point clear about its necessity for this battle.

Chapter 1 – Study Guide

1. Pilar heard about God since she was a child, from her parents and grandparents.

2. Do you think this is why she was able to trust God all through her life as an adult, even when her life was at stake?

3. Do you know of someone who trusted God regardless of life?

    a. Think on, and/or discuss how it affected your walk of faith.

Notes:

Chapter 2 – Another Damascus Fall

The Lord trains, and corrects those whom have been
given to Him because of Love, Hebrews 12:5-6.

Three people were standing in an empty warehouse on the second floor. The room was approximately the size of one-half of a football field. The walls and floor were various shades of light gray. The area was so bright it was as though the sun were shining through a multitude of windows.

Jesus, myself and a third-party, whom I somehow knew to be my guardian angel, conversed as we walked around. Suddenly, Jesus said He would be back. He turned and walked away. After a lengthy passage of time, I asked my guardian angel where was Jesus. He reassured me and said Jesus would be back. We waited for what seemed hours. Jesus had not yet returned.

Wait on the LORD and be of good courage, and He shall reinforce your true mind with His Strength.

Psalms 27: 14

Impatience, one of my old nemesis returned.

The search for an exit revealed a staircase towards the back of the warehouse. It included a chair lift. Unaware that I was about to fail a divine arranged test, it automatically started moving downward after I sat down. Suddenly, Jesus appeared to my right, as though He were walking on air. Like an arrow shot from a bow, joy catapulted me out of the chair as I jumped and reached towards Him across an expanse that looked like only a few feet. Instead, I fell *straight down* in a full free fall. At the bottom, when I looked up, it seemed as though I was gazing up at Jesus from a vast distance below where He stood.

"I didn't get hurt, I didn't get hurt," I kept stuttering in amazement at the distance I had fallen.

Suddenly, we were in a different part of the building where Jesus revealed the purpose of what I call my *Damascus Fall*. Regardless of my *spiritual* error, He had kept Satan from destroying me.

Then He gave me my assignment. I was commissioned to write for Him to encourage His sheep. But training was necessary. No longer surprised at the appearance of Jesus, I was yet dumbfounded at how I had gotten so far off the path.

Jesus said - No matter what, no one, nor demon, nor anything, or anyone, can snatch my sheep out of my hands, or the Fathers.

John 10: 27-30

The Word of God is clear. Those who are raised in the knowledge of God fare better with tests than those who were not. For instance, King David and Joseph, and others, held on to their faith in God in situations that would have destroyed many. On the other hand, Abraham was raised by a family that believed in pagan gods. Thus, it took him longer before his faith was strong like that of Joseph.

Pilar was raised since childhood knowing that God was a loving God. More specifically, because of her upbringing, she knew that God would hear her.

My journey is more likened to Abraham. Over and over, Jesus had to encourage me until I understood not only who He was, but who I am to Him and my purpose in His kingdom. This vision was just one of many where He had to step in and do a hands-on help.

This vision in the warehouse took place approximately six years after my spiritual rebirth. The relevance came a few years later. Shades of Abraham.

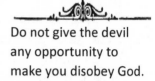

Do not give the devil any opportunity to make you disobey God.

Ephesians 4: 26-27

At the time, I was fighting to keep a building structure, *that I could not financially afford*. The first judge had ruled against me. In addition, it was revealed that people that I trusted had betrayed

our friendship. The second ruling on the appeal was about to take place. The night before the judge would issue his decision, Jesus gave me His ruling.

My pursuit of this building had created a rift in my faith walk.

Upon waking, the memory of the message of the dream was both exhilarating and devastating. Exhilarating because I had received an assignment directly from Jesus. Devastated because as close as I thought I was to Him, He showed me just the opposite.

How could I be that far from Him when I was doing God's work, I silently mused. After all, I am feeding and clothing the homeless and hungry, while ministering His Word to them.

He gave no further answer. He didn't have to. It was up to me to search through past events to find the beginning of the bread crumb trail that would explain my *Humpty-Dumpty* fall.

The Word of God revealed the answer. Unknowingly, I had violated His command.

Given the *unnatural* manner in which the building was acquired—no money down [at first], along with the *unusual* help that miraculously appeared to help me with renovation, I was convinced that a window from heaven had opened. Thus, taking back this building would be *taking back* what belonged to God.

My I.P.S. system was yet immature if not non-operational.

The ringing of the phone brought me out of my reverie of the past. The judge's ruling was in.

At 10 am, the hammer fell.

"It is my decision that regardless of any fraud you feel the owner committed, it is my ruling that you cannot afford this building, therefore my decision is in favor of the building owner," the judge stated. "And, you have 30 days to return the building to him."

My lawyer sat mute. Fists balled up at my side, eyes squinted and glaring, I leaned forward over the pedestal stand. Not even common sense could hold in the anger that was bubbling up from the pit of my stomach.

"Did you even bother to look at my evidence that shows that the owner committed fraud?" I demanded.

"It doesn't matter," he arrogantly replied.

Rage such as I had never experienced before rose up from the pit of my stomach and threatened to erupt like volcanic lava.

My unspoken thought of "how dare you" must have penetrated his head between his thick bushy gray eyebrows because his eyes widened as he looked down at me.

Lips clamped tighter than an unopened jar of pickles, I snapped to attention like a soldier in the military and spun around on my heels and silently walked out of the courtroom. Unaware that God was freeing me from an ungodly burden, I yet knew that if I said anything, the words that would pour out of my mouth would be ugly and non-retractable. However, at home that night, I did something really stupid.

God let me know that although He was my Father and I was His child, He was still Almighty God Supreme. The story of Job explains.

A few years back, the Holy Spirit had led me three times to study the book of Job. Twice I obeyed. The third time, I informed Him that I *knew* the lesson.

I did not.

The message that I had missed was that I must be vigilant to bind myself, my total dependence for everything in my lives to God, thru prayer. That we do not live *independently without God*. Every test is to see where we are as to whom we rely upon. In other words, the test checks us out whether we are relying upon our own *self*-strength. Our heart is indeed willing, but our human nature, our passion, is frail and strengthless, without the underlying foundational strength of our provider.

Tears welled up in my eyes and poured down my face at the thought of disappointing my Lord Jesus. On the other hand, His encouragement led me to a different height in obedience. What surprised me even more was that my assignment would be what I used to dream of as a child. Daydreams which I thought had died a final death when I was a teenager.

Once upon a time I was an avid reader of any kind of book. The desire to write stories about love and heroes who rescued damsels in distress rose up due to life with my mother. However, as far as I knew, that desire had died along with my concept of self-value.

Thereafter, having spent most of my adult life working as a secretary, law clerk, and office manager, I thought I knew how to write. The passage of time from when this assignment was given, to the publication of my first book, would reveal that I did not. Education was needed.

Enrollment in a variety of classes gave me a true insight into my true writing capability. There were so many red marks on my first paper from the college instructor that it looked like it was hemorrhaging. Writing tutors were available to the students. I immediately enrolled. Elizabeth E. was the best that I have ever come across.

She commented that I wrote like I talked using long and lengthy sentences. Rather than simply accept her corrections, I requested her aid in understanding how she was able to use shorter sentences to make the same point as my extra-long sentences. In conjunction with my English instructor, she taught me that writing has a beat to it like a piece of music. A class in poetry also taught this point.

Can two walk together, except they have agreed to do so?

Amos 3:3

Time would prove that writing for Jesus is not an easy task. It takes time and dedication to make sure that what we write is true. Take for instance the innumerable variations of God's word which we call the Bible. More so, when one considers the uncountable commentaries,

The Holy Spirit of God, who is His Spirit of Truth, is our teacher, and will bring to our memory the teachings of Jesus, thus our Holy Father. **John 14: 26; John 15: 26.**

and the various points of view, a true writer for God must rely upon the Holy Spirit for the truth of what we write.

It was a daunting task, but one I grew to love.

Intimidating because I knew the importance of what I had to write. Nevertheless, when I did the *Damascus* long-distance fall in the dream and did not get hurt, Jesus was assuring me that I was safe in his hands. He had not abandoned me despite my waywardness.

He had told me to wait. This instruction to wait is given numerous times throughout his word.

Abraham, who was 75 years of age at the time, had received a promise from Yahweh as to the blessings from his seed that God had in store for him. However, Abraham still thought that people could kill him. Scripture reveals that he had his wife Sarah lie and say she was not his wife. Then again, he and Sarah his wife, instead of waiting on God because 25 years had passed without the blessing coming to fruition, decided to help God out by having a child with another woman.

In all of these situations, the promise of God was not nullified, only delayed.

That day in the warehouse, my impatience got the better of me, as it often did with the biblical saints. When Jesus did not reappear according to *my* time schedule, I took matters into my own hands. I had yet to learn to wait both in cheerful expectation and hope.

Understanding came later regarding the decision. Jesus was setting me free—through the unrighteous acts of the judge—from an ungodly financial burden as well as people.

The doing of *good* works had made me believe that I was in His good graces. The *fall* showed me otherwise. Spiritually, I was in an agreement with the devil.

In *Ephesians 4: 21-23,* the King James Version translates *anastrophe as conversation.* However, most versions use it in place of *behavior.* One commentator translates these verses as follows: If we have listened to Jesus, and have been taught His truth, we have also learned to put aside our old manner of living where we relied upon our self. Thereafter, we were renewed in the spirit of our mind.

In other words, our behavior gives us away regardless of what we claim with our mouths.

A key word in these scriptures is *if,* verse 21. *If* we have not truly listened to Jesus with the intent to obey, then how can we change, according to verses 22-23. *Attitude* is the action of the old man. However, when the new man changes, our attitude, our altitude, *our position with Jesus,* also changes.

We are made in God's image and likeness. When the *body of Christ, the true church,* are gossiping, nit-picking, using profanity, we are presenting a worldly image to all. And it isn't pretty.

When the Holy Spirit begins His work in us, we are like corroded pennies that have lain outside in the weather. We are covered with muck, filth, and corrosion. In order to clean the penny, it has to be dunked in acid. Some are so corroded that they need to be dunked twice, or three times, like me.

We must examine ourselves, and the position of our faith. If not, the devil will check us out to see if we are relying upon ourselves, or Jesus.

Galatians 5: 24

But, beneath lies the original creation.

For the *body of Christ,* as my Damascus fall illustrates, adversity is the acid-bath of correction. The scriptures are the horse-hair bristle scrub brush for our souls.

Apostle Paul considered his body as an enemy with which he must contend. My *continuous* mistakes made me want to beat up my own body as well. Why would anyone listen to *my* words about the saving grace of God's Word, *if* it *looks like* it has no authority in my life.

The Word was working *in me,* but I was still a work in progress, as the *fall* clearly indicated. I had to learn how to stop letting the devil trick me into disobeying Jesus.

Like Eve, I *thought* I was doing a good thing. After all, I was feeding the hungry and clothing those that needed clothing. In addition, I was teaching and talking about His eternal love and His Words that we, His creation, are valuable. However, in order to do these things, I had gotten into bed with the devil through an extensive amount of debt because I *failed* to follow God's specific commands of operation.

Despite the effect on my ego, my fall included first encouragement as we walked around the warehouse and talked. Then, came the test of my trust in His Word that He would be back. In that He knows all things, Jesus knew I would fail and fail due to my impatience in waiting on Him. This was needed to show me how far I was from Him. Then, after He recovered His silly child, He assured me that I was in His hands and no one could snatch me out of His hand, thus His authority. Last, He gave me my eternal assignment.

So, despite my error, and still needing more training, my eternal purpose in His kingdom plans remained intact.

His manner of handling a wayward child gave me pause to wonder. Just maybe Eve was also a work in progress who had to *learn* how to handle the eternal assignment that God had spoken into her life, and thus every woman. And, the devil *knew* the importance of that special anointing. This explains why women are the target of Satan around the world.

Just maybe, *the Fall* was all about growing up and understanding who we really are in the kingdom of Jesus Christ. And, the importance of knowing what *thus saith the Lord, only.*

Chapter 2 Study Guide

1. Do you know anyone that seemed on the right track and suddenly they lost everything?

    a. Were they able to explain what happened?

    b. Did they know how they missed the mark?

    c. Did they correct their error?

2. How do you see the mistake?

3. Did it change your faith walk? How? Discuss.

Notes:

Chapter 3 – A Weed Sprouts in the Garden

Weeds are destructive. In order to not harm the baby plant, both must grow up together until the intended plant is ready for harvest. Then the weed will be destroyed. Matthew 13: 24-30.

Awedding was scheduled. God wanted the location to be a one-of-a-kind. He decided it would take place in a special created Garden.

First, God brought forth the future husband to prepare the Garden prior to his new wife's arrival. After the rain, the rich brown and black earth, warm from the unblemished rays of the sun, brought forth plants and trees that not only looked good, but would serve as food for the couple.

Jesus teaches His believers about gardening, and the danger of spiritual weeds of disbelief,

Matthew 13: 1-50

Personally, I have no doubt that many lush plants, multicolored flowers, and fruit trees, perfumed the air. The aroma of blooming orange blossoms comes to mind.

Rather than musical instruments or drums, the melodious sound of a multitude of a variety of birds and animals must have supplied the melody. Always a God of order, He created a river that was directed to irrigate the Garden.

It had to be a beautiful day.

It is not difficult to assume that the bride-to-be was a starry-eyed lady who believed that she knew the path to her destiny. The outlook for her new life could only get better.

However, anyone who is familiar with gardening is aware that weeds have a tendency to sneak in and sprout. In this case, the weed was the enemy of God and mankind.

According to scripture, Satan already had a history of exceeding power in being wicked and evil. He draws near the woman, each step determined, careful, and pre-planned. His conversation starts with a question. He gives the newly wed Eve the impression that he is seeking wisdom from her. His voice strong yet strangely calming, he asks her for information. He suggests that she is not thinking high enough of herself.

She rejects his philosophy. More so, she adds that not only must they not eat of this *knowledge,* they are not to even touch it. However, the devil doesn't give up. He uses a *mind-altering vision* to convince Eve that *his* knowledge is *as good as God's spiritual food.* Eve fails to comprehend that she has been studied, much like an animal of prey that is circled by a stalker just before the kill.

This not so free exchange of knowledge changed the world. Evil became normal, something that *looks* good, and will make one *wise* in all that is ungodly. And, the benefits, *greed, gold, possessions,* make it palatable.

It remains the same today. Drugs, alcohol, ungodly sexual relationships, and worse, are all made to *look* and *feel* good to make them appetizing. Satan has not changed his agenda.

The *Dream Killer* had gone for the jugular of Eve's godly mission. She never saw it coming.

Have you been on the *receiving* end of a *lovingly* made suggestion to choose, and complied? The chaos that followed your choice forced you to question your sanity. You rage with anger, sometimes *silently,* feeling *betrayed.* Another relationship bites the dust.

With *different standards*—or so you believed--you *choose* the same *type* of man that betrayed you the first time. We wonder, *now how did that happen?*

Jesus said it is His Word that brings us back to life because His words are spirit and they are alive.

John 6: 63

What about *your* suggestions, made out of the kindness of your heart? Was there confusion in that person's life following your suggestion?

Personally, before God intervened in my life, I thought I knew that God *didn't* exist. This lie from hell was the result of the devastating horror of childhood. Therefore, the claims of Christians about God's existence and His Eternal *love,* were ridiculous. The abuser in my life was a professing Christian.

From the beginning of my faith journey, it was normal to hear professing believers talk about being saved. However, what I *saw* were familiar ungodly behaviors from my former world of disbelief. The question was *why* and *how* could that be? Time, and the embracing of God's Word, revealed that Satan was truly the culprit. It made sense of my own actions of continually tripping and falling as a new spiritual child.

Prior to spiritual rebirth, the question often arose in *how* had *I* become everything mother had spoken in my ears when I was a child. Time proved that although it was yet to come true, the devil—through her—had actually spoke into *the gate to my soul,* as to what I would become. Thus, from the age of 16 until I met my second husband, I was a walking and talking image of everything that I had hated in my mother.

For instance, my mother repeatedly *spoke into my soul* that I was good for nothing. The result is that for most of my life, I acted the part. Men were allowed to misuse me because I had no sense of self-value.

The realization of the negative impact that the words of my mother had made in my life made me grasp the danger of what I had spoken into the lives of my children.

Jesus said that the words that *He speaks* are spirit and life. And, because they are *alive*, they are like spiritual food and water to our souls. Life has a way of proving this truth.

Jesus told the first disciples that they were clean through the Word that He had spoken to them. Plainly, the true Word of God is a mental bath for our minds.

John 15:3

My daughter told me that as a child her father always stated in my absence that he was the only one who loved her. And, that I did *not* love her. Through the influence of the devil, my mother had emotionally separated my younger brothers through the same method.

In other words, the ungodly spirit of my mother had been in my first husband.

There is an old saying that sometimes in life, when we are trying to avoid correction, we tend to jump from the frying pan and into the fire. Clearly, with the choice of my first husband, I had jumped right into the fire.

God mended our mother and daughter relationship.

It is written that Satan copies or mimics everything that God does to make himself, and his disciples, look like light. The *spoken* true Word of God washes our souls/our hearts as it cleans us up. Could this be why Satan goes to so much trouble to have words spoken into our ears that are in complete contrast to God's truth?

According to scriptures, the disciples had been under the process of cleansing purification all the time that they had been with Jesus. Gradually, their *way of thinking* returned back to God's original design and purpose which He had declared.

In the natural, branches on trees and plants, that are not bearing fruit, are pruned, i.e. cut off. Spiritually, it is the same.

In our new way of thinking, i.e. repent, we *cut off* our former way of thinking. In turn, this changes our behavior and allows our lives to proceed into the future in a new direction.

God's words speak life into our souls. In contrast, what is the effect of Satan's words of unworthiness? We do not have to guess. Today, every form of media broadcasts the results.

Children are committing suicide because someone *said* that they didn't like them, or they were ugly, etc. Satan will do all he can to make sure we hear words that produce death.

Words are either of life or death,

Proverbs 18: 21 [a]

The battle is with the devil.

Jesus trained the disciples for survival. He knew what they, *thus You and I,* His true Church, would endure. Training initiates the removal of our *old ungodly* desires including lifelong patterns and choices.

Thinking of quitting. Beware! Quitting will keep you in the place you've always been.

Embedded truth will launch you into your future, delivered from bondage, free! As a battle-scarred victor, our *past* is the first rung on the ladder to victory in Jesus.

God's revelation of His existence—during my spiritual rebirth—also introduced me to the *new* me, which was actually the *original* me that was first created by God. In contrast, the *old* me had been shaped and formed by the demonically influenced words of unworthiness, spoken by my mother.

The revelation of God, that informed me that there was a *different* me buried beneath the *old* familiar me, was stunning. Likewise, the knowledge that I had been destined before my birth for my assignment was life-changing.

I know. I hope however that the incorrect vernacular of English makes the seriousness of this point clear. The goal of Satan remains the same, from the Garden of Eden, to today, as illustrated in the stories in *We Are One*. He desires that we are *never* to understand the importance of our existence.

God Said that Rulers will arise on earth and *think* to change the times and laws that God put in place. And, for a time, they will be allowed to do so.

Daniel 7:24-25; 2: 20-21.

The funny thing is that before I knew God, I would often inform Christian friends that hell was here on earth. I had no idea that I was speaking a truth.

Have you ever watched a parent grab a child in the collar? The child doesn't view the discipline as love, but with that one hand the child is shaken, chastised, and at the same time held or pulled out of danger. Given my assignment, sometimes God needed to collar me as He chastised me and kept me away from danger. I truly believe that God does have a sense of humor?

God's revelation of my *true* identity initiated the collapse of my former understanding of *who* I thought I was with a resounding roar. In turn, God's undeniable truth revealed the hidden, insidious, methodology of the devil. And, Satan, who also did not exist in my mind, was Johnny-on-the-spot. He sucker-punched me with the awareness of his existence within 12 hours of God's revelation.

Between the two revelations, everything that I thought I knew, everything that I had based my lifelong choices upon, was shattered. The world nurtures and trains people to blame other people as the culprit for the disasters in their lives. I followed suit. The chaos in my life was never due to my own choices. However, once God shows us His truth, shouldn't our choices be better?

Yes. But it is a process.

The passage of time reveals that the enemy has many faces but no specific gender. *We Are One* demonstrates this truth through the various stories.

A woman's lack of knowledge of self-worth, especially as to our godly purpose, is the breeding ground for practically every negative action. This deficiency is the source, or better yet, the foundation that influences the world.

In plain English, the devil uses men and women, who are unaware of their divine value, as the ministers to achieve his goal of destruction throughout all generations. The result is that soul-injured people breed soul-injured seed.

Social media outlets blast this horrendous truth on a daily basis.

The devil is serious about his job. His methods still work today. Neither the pattern nor the purpose of his goal has changed. Why? It still works. And, his purpose crosses all lines of color, religion and nationality.

People's choices are impenetrable until the knowledge of their *godly* value and purpose is changed. Thus, mankind is unable to alter their knowledge of self-worth absent the involvement of the one who gave it to us in the first place.

An erroneous concept, even among the religious community, is that people rise in the morning and determine that they will serve Satan. That is *not* what God said. However, that is exactly what we do daily, due to our perverted knowledge of self-worth and purpose.

In my past life absent God's truth, my choices were believed to be good ones. Life clearly demonstrated the opposite.

Why does a woman accept, take on and absorb every act of violence committed against her, as though it's her destiny? She is physically beat and concludes that she is unworthy. She is raped and concludes she did the enticing. She is verbally attacked and challenged as to her intellectual worth and yet concludes that there is something wrong with her.

It is written that God said it is by lack of knowledge *of His Ways and Truth* that we are destroyed. And, we go into captivity because of this lack of knowledge.

Hosea 4: 6; Isaiah 5: 13.

Why and where is this transference for responsibility birthed? What is the goal beneath the unspoken but firm belief that it's always the woman?

Ladies we are and have been in a war from the beginning. We've been on the frontline of the battle, without proper preparation, because of our true purpose.

Army recruits are trained prior to battle. Boxers and football teams check out their opponents before the match or game? A wise business person first researches their competition prior to competing in the same field.

Failure to research and acquire training before combat always results in defeat. God did *not* send us into battle unprepared. His battle plan has always been in His Word. Yet, why are women still ill-prepared for the most important battle of all?

The enemy has made sure—through his followers—that God's Word about our mission was reinvented and *hidden in plain sight.* The result is that women have been left trying to fight in the wrong way. More importantly, women, mothers-to-be, would not know how to teach their daughters, their sisters, and their sons, of the importance of *living in Purpose* to God's will.

We are One removes the mask off of God's truth.

As the designer of our mission, God is serious about our growing up into our role. He proved this point by allowing me to take that *Humpty-Dumpty* fall down a *spiritual rabbit hole.* Yet, because of His everlasting love for us, He did not allow my break-neck somersault to shatter me into unfixable portions. Instead, it reinforced the certainty in my heart and soul about the importance of my mission. In addition, it encouraged me as to the faithfulness of His promise that we are safe in His hands, i.e. His authority. It instilled a steel-like determination to learn how to truly walk this path and learn who we, *the woman,* are according to God.

Oftentimes, children spend their entire lives searching out parents who gave them away. Siblings search for missing brothers and sisters.

The need to know our identity is like a hunger that is gnawing away at our insides. What the world has missed is that this *appetite* is spiritual. And, the devil does everything he can to make sure we never discover the reason this knowledge is so essential. Nevertheless, the devil fails, again and again, because God always has His people in place to bring forth His truth and mission in the life of a woman, as in this next story.

Chapter 3 Study Guide

Over the centuries, a multitude of scenarios have been suggested, and invented, about how Eve got tricked by the devil. What is seldom discussed is the fact that Satan went into her mind and gave her a vision that 'tricked" her into seeing evil as good, etc.

1. Do you think this is possible? Discuss.

Notes:

Chapter 4 – Cinderella's Carriage

Arrived on Time

Our heavenly Father gives us good things
when we ask [in Faith], Matthew 7: 11

Once upon a time, there lived an unhappy young girl. She was sad for her mother didn't like her one little bit. Cinderella was the child of her husband who was dead. All the nice things, kind thoughts and loving touches were for the other children. And not just the kind thoughts and love, but also dresses, shoes, shawls, delicious food, comfy beds, as well as every home comfort. But for the poor unhappy first child, there was nothing at all. No lovely prepared meals. Oftentimes, not even scraps. It was left up to Cinderella to clean up behind the others. After all the work was done, Cinderella was allowed to sit for a while by the fire, near the cinders in the fireplace. That is how she got her nickname in the fairy tale.

Gwendolyn Madison's life is similar to Cinderella's story. There are only a few differences.

Unlike the fairy tale character, Gwendolyn, African-American, 67 years of age, was her mother's natural child. And she was her first child. But in many other instances, she was treated like *Cinderella*. Her mother disliked her so much that she found it impossible to treat her with love and kindness. However, her mother was able to love her other children who came later.

Like *Cinderella*, Gwendolyn had to work hard. First at school and then at home. It was her job to clean up after the entire family. She grew up in church since the age of two. Her mother took her to service every Sunday. She remembers the messages of fire and brimstone which were normal in the 50s and 60s.

At around the age of 12, Gwendolyn was baptized because it was the thing to do. All the children were christened at around the same age. The children and family were very active in church. They had Wednesday night Bible study. The children were at church when their mother was in choir practice. The entire family participated in religious service at least three days a week. But God was never discussed outside of church. Nor did her mother ever pick up a Bible once they left the building on Sundays.

Gwendolyn's mother remarried when she was around six and a half years old. The last name of Gwendolyn's father was Johnson. The remarriage gave a different last name to all the rest of her siblings.

Around the age of eleven, Gwendolyn realized that her mother never hugged her or any of the children.

God said teach the children [about Him] in the morning, noon, and night,

Deuteronomy 6: 6-7

Her stepdad was the nurturer of the family. At first, she did not realize that he was not her birth father. Eventually, other family members told her the truth. He also was the cook in the family. Her mother never cooked.

"It was never physical abuse," Gwendolyn stated. "Instead, even as a child I could sense her dislike of just me."

Rejection was enforced by other means. She was forced as a teenager to take a bath in her brother's dirty bath water. This behavior only stopped when Gwendolyn told a teacher, who then called her mother. Finally, for the first time in years, Gwendolyn was allowed to bath in clean water.

Her mother never apologized or explained her behavior. Worse, the siblings who were loved picked up on their mother's hatred of their sister.

Nevertheless, every Sunday the family was in church.

"I don't remember hearing any messages about faith or self-value, or forgiveness," Gwendolyn said. "Instead punishment sermons, fire and brimstone and burning in hell, were taught."

Gwendolyn grew up in the latter 40s and 50s. This seems to have been the normal message in religious services at that time. Gwendolyn said she never gave much thought to the comparison of how her mother treated her in relationship with her church attendance.

When they started attending another church, there was a separate church for the youth. The ten Commandments, the story of Joseph, Noah and the Ark, and Adam and Eve were studied. However, they were never taught messages about virtue, faith, or value.

Church was entertainment.

Gwendolyn became pregnant with her first child, a daughter, at age 15. The father was a neighbor. She had never been taught about her female body.

This is understandable. The godly functions of a woman's body were literally considered a disgrace by many women during this time.

Initially, her mother told her she could stay at home and have the baby. Without warning, her mother decided she had to get married and get out of her house. She was 16.

"I had no idea of what it meant to be a wife much less a mother," Gwendolyn said.

She had to drop out of school because you could not be pregnant in those times and attend school. Thereafter, she was shunned by both friends and their parents. Although she was married, even her close girlfriends stayed away.

Separated from family and friends she had no one with whom she could communicate. She was informed by her mother not to come over during the daytime because neighbors would see that she was pregnant.

Many years later, Gwendolyn found her mother's marriage certificate. It showed the date that her mother and father had married. She discovered that her mother was pregnant with Gwendolyn prior to marriage.

"When I became pregnant, my mother made it seem as though I were the most sinful person in the world," Gwen stated. "To find out that she had done the same thing made me so angry. She and my father had been intimate while in high school. She had always presented herself as a priceless pure Christian. She admitted the truth when I confronted her."

Still, her mother never apologized for her treatment of her daughter, according to Gwendolyn.

Prior to their marriage, Gwendolyn knew her husband as the boy across the street. He was a few years older than she was. He married her because her mother threatened him. Her husband was in his early 20s.

"I never thought he would abuse me, but I had seen his violent temper," she said. "He had got into a fight with another man to protect me. I thought that was a cool thing."

During her pregnancy, Gwendolyn was isolated from everyone. She now lived over 30 minutes away from her family. She was shunned by church people that she had known for years. She was left with only her husband for companionship. Her days consisted of waiting on him to come home. But, at the same time, she was scared of him.

Her godmother, a church member, took Gwendolyn under her wing.

"I was breaking out in hives from head to toe from nerves," Gwendolyn said.

My godmother came to the house one day and packed me up and took me to her house. I was still pregnant with my first baby and crying all the time because I had no one to talk to. Her godmother had children.

"I got a chance to be a child again and play games with her children," Gwendolyn said. "She contacted my mother and chastised her for forcing me to get married."

Gwendolyn is one of many women who were practically forced into adulthood while still a child. In the 50s and early 60s, people still confronted each other about their children. This was a blessing for Gwendolyn. If not for neighbors and teachers that God used to intervene in her behalf, life for Gwendolyn might have been even worse.

Take for instance, the godmother who knew Gwendolyn from church. She confronted Gwendolyn's mother about her treatment of her daughter. She then took it upon herself to teach Gwendolyn that she had the ability to make choices for her own life.

In another situation, a teacher called her mother because Gwendolyn was always tired in school. Gwendolyn had explained that she always had to go home and clean the house. And, that there was seldom any food left for her. Afterward, without explanation or an apology, she was allowed to come home and do homework first before housework. And, sometimes, there would be scrapings of food left for her to eat.

In other words, her mother changed to keep up the appearance to the world that she was a godly person and mother. Gwendolyn believes that her stepfather did not know that her mother was not feeding her.

Gwendolyn's mother eventually moved to Detroit with her husband and the rest of the family when Gwendolyn's daughter was barely a year old. Thus, her children did not have a grandmother who was close. Meanwhile, her second child Norman died from a crib death.

Her husband was livid when she became pregnant again. She was supposedly on the pill. But, in her mind, it wasn't that essential.

"I really did not understand the true importance and purpose of the pill," she stated.

Gwendolyn said she is not surprised at how her children turned out. She was raised in a negative atmosphere. She knew nothing else. She admits therefore that her children experienced the same from her. I understand.

At one time, the world called the lost, disobedient, children the generation X. And, proclaimed that their behavior was unexplainable.

The Word of God repeatedly gives the answer to the existence of dysfunctional children. Nothing happens by chance. When true *godly* love is not in the mix, the opposite spirit controls the house and all who are in it, as the other stories in *We Are One* reveal.

The death of her son through crib death was devastating. Gwendolyn said she did not understand death.

"I remember just sitting at the mortuary and staring at him," she said. He looked like he was sleeping. His death did not make sense."

Gwendolyn was a teenager when her son died. I was considerably beyond that age when my second husband died. His death did not make sense. Both Gwendolyn and I were sitting on church pews, listening to weekly messages, and yet were clueless about what happens when we die.

God left the truth in His Word. However, what *Thus Saith the Lord* about our earthly lives seems to be a secret as ministers around the world claim the holiness of the departed one, regardless of the real life they lived.

Gwendolyn decided that her children had to be her first priority, unlike the treatment she received from her mother. For instance, when she was barely a teenager, she had to catch a bus to school at 6 A.M. when it was still dark.

"My mother never got up with me to make sure I was safe," she stated.

One morning a child molester stopped his car and tried to get Gwendolyn to get into his car. She said no. He started to get out of the car. She started screaming and ran home and told her mother. She was in the eighth grade. She was 13. The police came by and took a description. Her mother finally asked the bus driver to stop directly at their house and pick up Gwendolyn.

On the other hand, Gwendolyn said that her mother always got up with the other kids and fixed breakfast for them.

"I never felt protected," Gwendolyn said. "I could see that the other children were treated differently, which I never understood. I could not figure out what I had done to make her hate me the way she did."

The Word of God, and personal experience, reveals that the negative *past* is like the teeth of an animal trap, albeit invisible. A current women's movement is a prime example of this truth. The ancient hurts and acts of abuse lock onto our hearts and souls for years. It is destructive. It is generational because it is passed on to the new seed, the children, like a *spiritual* HIV infection.

The life of Gwendolyn Madison exemplifies this truth.

She knew something was wrong even as a child. Although she had been in church most of her life, she has not discussed it because the concept of *don't look back to the past* is a foundation in most religious communities. On the other hand, the natural world in which we live demonstrates a different reality.

For instance, in construction, when a builder is notified that something has gone wrong with a building, they look back in the past to see what happened. Why? The error is in the past. And, unless the mistake is corrected, the future longevity of that structure is jeopardized.

Gwendolyn did not want to be rejected yet again.

God's answer to my questions as to why and how do we as women continue to repeat the same mistakes was simple and biblical. He sent me to the origin of our beginnings.

The Holy Spirit revealed that our future is in understanding *the past*. This actuality is utilized in the scriptural stories about Jesus. Yahovah explained the path that Jesus must take in the Old Testament. The OT also explains where it began as to how the devil *so* successfully deceived the woman, and thus every woman today.

Her mother died in 2018. Shortly thereafter, God revealed the mystery of the hostile relationship between Gwendolyn and her mother.

Our lives are not a surprise to God. Gwendolyn loved her mother despite how she had been treated by the woman who gave birth to her. It is often the case. Surprisingly, while sharing her grief with a friend over the loss of her mother, the Holy Spirit revealed the answer.

The explanation as to why Gwendolyn was disliked by her mother was in the past.

Her mother's pregnancy with Gwendolyn had changed the path of her mother forever. Women were not allowed to remain in the Army while pregnant. And despite years of sitting on a church pew, she had never forgiven Gwendolyn for altering her life.

The ungodly spirit of a woman's lack of value started with her grandmother, according to Gwendolyn. To her knowledge, this demonic concept was passed on to her mother. However, her mother fought to achieve a purpose and some sort of recognition that would guarantee that she was worthy. She ran away from home and city and joined the Army.

Over the passage of time, Gwendolyn discovered that she was imitating her mother by disassociating herself from people that professed their dislike of her. Like her mother, she always claimed belief in God. Yet, she had never heard of her purpose in the kingdom of God until she attended a woman's conference that was hosted by a well-known, plain-talking, female speaker.

Throughout the majority of her life, her mother would negatively talk against Gwendolyn to all the other family members. When questioned, her mother would apologize and then repeat the same behavior.

Church life was a viable part of Gwendolyn's life. However, love, value, and forgiveness, were never discussed until she listened to the pastor of the church that she now attends.

Satan's goal has never changed from the beginning to today. His intent is to kill, steal, and destroy, mankind. Thus, he uses family members to instigate *generational genocide,* which includes using the devastating events of life to teach a woman that she has no value.

No one will ever know what great purpose God had in store for Gwendolyn's mother. What we do know from Gwendolyn's story is that when her mother's run for freedom came to a screeching halt due to pregnancy, hatred replaced love.

Satan had Gwendolyn on the same path.

Nevertheless, when God says enough is enough, it is done.

The exposure of the *root* of hate set Gwendolyn free. For years, she had believed that it was the average circumstances of life that had caused her mother's behavior. Now, she is aware that it had nothing to do with her personally. Her mother hated being poor thus her flight to the Army. She hated being considered valueless. Serving her country would have given her value.

Gwendolyn had heard constantly that Jesus loved her, but her life contradicted what she heard. It left her confused. Now her life is on a different track.

"I was stunned at God's revelation," she said. "I now understand that I am pre-destined for a godly purpose rather than to be merely a servant to people."

In other words, Gwendolyn's story is proof that it is never too late to find your purpose and *live* in it.

The story of Cinderella ends with a declaration to the prince that she was a good and patient person.

From personal experience, Gwendolyn is a kind and loving person who reaches out even to strangers. I am one of them. When we first met a few years ago, she physically and spiritually embraced me and made me feel welcome in her life.

Satan loses again.

We never know what a person has endured. Those who know Gwendolyn would never guess at the turmoil of her past life because she never openly discusses it. She did for this book that women around the world can know that Satan is on his job even in this era.

Awareness of the root cause of the past always has a wondrous effect on the recipient. Gwendolyn's Faith in Jesus and her trust in God—as to her value—has been restored. She knows she is essential in the kingdom of Jesus Christ. Gwendolyn is stronger and standing firmly on the *Rock*.

Her I.P.S. system is now functioning.

But for others, as in the following chapter, they are still lost in the devil's maze of confusion, fear, and anger.

Chapter 4 Study Guide

1. Children are precious gifts to mankind from God. However, as this story reveals, this truth has gotten lost.

   a. What do you believe is the reason?

2. Have you been involved with a friend that grew up in a religious community but under this type of condemnation from a parent?

   a. Did you understand their dilemma at the time?

   b. What happened to that person? Discuss.

Notes:

Chapter 5 – A 21ˢᵗ Century Job Spirit

In order to produce fruit, branches must be trimmed, John 15: 2

Each woman sways quietly to the worship music, eyes tightly closed, arms lifted in worship. Salty tears seep from beneath lowered eyelids. Muted whispers of Hallelujah, Hallelujah, Hallelujah, can be heard from all three. One is Caucasian. Another is Creole and Caucasian. The third is African-American. All seems right in their lives as the daughters of Jesus. However, looks can be deceiving.

Each woman is so angry at the circumstances of their past that it has disfigured the face and body of each. All look older than their true years. Each was raised since childhood in their local respective churches. Yet, each has a story to tell that would break your heart. Neither of the three has yet to come to terms with the horror of their existence.

They are not alone. Through my travels, I have watched the repeat of this scenario from North to South, from East to West, and even out of the country. What is plain is that Satan does not mind women attending local churches as long as they do not believe what they hear about God's Eternal Love and Forgiveness.

God warned us about Satan and his tricks in the Bible. Thus, from first-hand experience, He also gave us the right information in how to stop the devil's influence in our lives.

It is clear that mere words alone do not work, or else there would not be so many people, especially women, still in bondage under Satan's influence. God's truth as to whom we belong must be implanted in our minds. It must be a part of us like our bones and tendons.

The pretense of faith is not unusual. This *fake* worship is biblical—if you will. And, although it is not easily perceived, it is known. In the book of Job, God knew of Job's inward doubts about Him. And, so did Satan. But *how* does the devil know when we are uncertain in our faith? In Job's case, we don't have to guess.

In the book of Job, Satan made a bargain with God to attack him because he claimed that he knew Job better than God. God said *go ahead,* but you cannot kill him. The devil said Job would curse God to his face. Eventually, Job did. Nevertheless, this scriptural fact is seldom preached.

The severity of the illness made Job challenge everything that God had made, just as Satan said. But, God is not pleased with Job's reaction.

Isaiah 45: 9-10.

Job did love God. He believed that God was Supreme. Then, he finally acknowledges that he *never trusted* God. In that God is never unjust, it is my opinion based on scripture that this is why God allowed the devil to destroy everything that Job owned.

Job admits that although he preached to others about being loved by God and being safe with him, he personally feared that he was never safe.

Job 3:25-26

In other words, Job's story is a warning about claiming to believe God, but inwardly, does not trust God. We need to be aware of our own faith journey.

Job needed to understand that faith is more than an intellectual position, which he came to understand from chapters

36 to the end. Specifically, in chapter 42, Job admits that he previously thought that he knew Yahovah. But after the misfortune of illness, he really does and he repented, i.e. thought different.

God said okay and returned everything back to Job.

Satan was so assured of his knowledge of Job that he was not swayed from his position even after the first two failures, and regardless of what God said about Job. The devil kept going back to Him to get permission to test Job. Then, he hit on the *right* challenge against faith. Personal tragedy on self.

In other words, Satan knows we *talk* a good story until persecution or illness becomes personal, such as the three women in this story.

However, few messages teach this scriptural truth about Job. Yet, *it is written* in the Word of God. Initially, even after he was covered with sores and boils, Job commented to his wife that receiving evil as well as good is part of obeying God. But, over the next several days, the illness became so severe that he finally opened his mouth and curses the day of his birth, and everything else that God had created. This included his mother, his father, the purpose of the stars in heaven, and more.

Job has now done exactly what Satan said he would do. But, how could the devil know this about Job unless he has a deeper knowledge of our mind and soul.

History reveals that this same type of persecution causes many to back away from God, such as the three women in this story. Add me in—as my book *Mine, an Everlasting Promise of Love, et al* demonstrates. That is until God opened my eyes to the purpose of adversity. My book, *Purposely Unchained* goes into specific detail.

During the time that I came to know the above three ladies, they shared the reasons for their heartache. What happened was tragic. For them, it is unrepairable. Nevertheless, it is not over until God says so. Only time will tell what God has in store for them.

How often do we mourn and pray for others that are suffering serious problems? We tell them give it to God and pray. Then, tragedy hits home on a personal level. Some maintain their faith. Others fall short.

God wants us to know His thoughts through His Word because it includes the road map that leads us to our identity and purpose. But, when scriptures are ignored because they don't fit within a particular religion, it denies God's truth to the hearers.

It is written that God left us His Word because He wants all generations to know His thoughts,

Psalms 33: 11

The usual erroneous teaching about Job is that he did not sin with his lips to wrongly accuse God of error. Not only does God's Word refute this blunder in Job 38, God personally challenges Job about his insubordination with a resume unlike any other. In addition, God reminds us that striving, i.e. disagreeing with the way that He, Yahovah, does things is not good. A personal experience brought all of these scriptures home to roost. I did the same thing approximately four to five years into my new life with Jesus.

God makes it clear that a human arguing with Him about life is not a good thing.

Isaiah 45: 9-10.

Job accused God of error. The author of this book—yes, me—did the same thing. And, like Job, I also got a paranormal whipping.

That particular night is *still* clear in

my memory. Satan stepped right up into my house as though he owned it. I hope to never forget it because God was letting me know that although He was my spiritual Father, He was still God.

What brought this chastisement about was my determination that a business loss should not have occurred. That night, I had announced in God's face, yes, that I would not pray to Him because I was so hurt and angry. Satan must have been rejoicing because I was doing the same thing as Job. But, the moment Satan appeared, my entire attitude changed along with my spiritual altitude.

Full obedience to God results in the devil fleeing,

James 4: 7

Remember as children when we suddenly were reminded that our parent was still in charge. Usually this took place after we were told to go get the belt or switch.

The appearance of Satan made me *remember* to whom I belonged.

Words about my God-identity started flowing from my mouth like microwaved hot syrup. Specifically, I told the devil, *no you didn't just waltz up into my house. You don't have anything coming here. Now get out. I belong to Jesus.*

All this while rolling my eyes and neck, you know ladies, to emphasize my position. Here is what happened.

Satan left. I knew I had messed up. Instead of sitting up and standing to my feet, I literally rolled out of bed onto my knees to praise and worship my Father and ask for forgiveness as I repented for my behavior.

Knowledge of the Word of God, and especially the book of Job, made it obvious that God had allowed Satan to come at me just as He had with Job. My heavenly Father got my attention.

Like Job, and the three women at the start of this chapter, I was continually proclaiming the goodness of God. But, when everything fell apart faster than an avalanche roaring down a mountain side, my behavior imitated Job.

Actions do speak louder than words.

Since God is not double-minded, were his actions justified with Job and I. Yes. We needed to *know* our hidden weakness.

Many profess to trust God. Our declaration will be tested.

Anger and pain at life's events open the door for Satan. Trust in God

Just as the rain and the snow obey Him, God said His commandments accomplish what He sent it to do,

Isaiah 55: 11

and love for Jesus closes that entrance. When the devil sees our *faith*, he leaves.

The lives of the three women bring to light the purpose of this book. Mothers need to know their essential *godly* importance in the lives of their children.

In contrast, in the lives of the three women, the damage inflicted to their souls by their mother's has left them unable to recover. Instead of God's words of love, hate was continually spoken into their ears, i.e. their souls.

Finally, I understood. We plant the seed. Others water the seed. But, in His time, God will cause His Word to produce fruit. Regardless of what I heard before my rebirth, words of transformation could not be perceived until God *opened* my spiritual ears.

God said His Word never comes back void. The key point is that it will have the desired effect when He sends it, and not when we send it.

On many occasions, *I* have been trying to help my friends with the Word of God without a direct command from the Father to do so. I stopped unless I *knew* I had a direct command to go forth with His Word.

As a called child by Yahovah and servant to Christ, my goal *must* be to become likeminded like Jesus. Thus, I must do as He did, which is to speak only what, where, and when God through His Holy Spirit tells me to speak. As for helping my children, whom I unknowingly taught the ways of the world, the Holy Spirit revealed the answer in how to help through the Word.

Jesus informs the believer that in order for a prayer to bear fruit, there are conditions. Oops! It was time to regroup and go back to the drawing board.

The *Greek* word for the English word *abide* holds the key. *Meno, Greek,* is a primary verb for abide. It means to stay in a given place, state, relation or expectancy with Jesus *by Faith*. But wait! There is a second part to this condition for answered prayers. His Word *must* [obligation, essential, duty] be *in* us. Plainly, we *must both know and believe* the Word, which in turn puts us into a relationship of Faith and expectancy in and with Jesus.

Paul was sent first to the non-Jewish nations, and kings and then the children of Israel. However, he went first to the Jewish synagogue,

Acts 9: 15, 20.

Jesus said that if we remain in a relationship with Him, **AND** His Word is the source of our Faith and expectancy in Him, whatever we ask, it shall be done,

John 15: 1-8

The movie *Eli* came to mind. Understanding required a second time of watching the movie. First of all, it is a violent movie. But, that aside, people were chasing the character to steal his book, the Bible. It finally dawned on me that there was no physical book. The *entire* Bible was in his head.

We must *know* the Word in our heart and mind. And, this takes *daily* study. After 24 years, I still do not know the entire Bible by heart. However, I have read it so many times that when I *hear* something that is contrary to God's Word, I know whether it is truth or error. And then there are the really special times that reminds me through His Word that it was *and is* He who kept me safe during certain events.

His Word *in me* allows me to pray for my family because through the knowledge of prayer, I will not pray for anything that is contrary to His Word. Jesus is adamant about what we do with His Word. The journey of Apostle Paul comes to mind.

Apostle Paul was given the assignment by Jesus to go to the non-Jewish people to first preach the Good News. Instead, Paul first spoke the gospel to his fellow Pharisees.

His behavior is understandable. He was Jewish, and a Pharisee. Through the influence of Jesus, he had come to understand that he had been mistaken about his beliefs about Him. Thus, Paul was determined to help his friends come to the same realization that Jesus Christ was the true Messiah.

Apostle Paul finally goes to the Gentiles, and God assures him of his safety because he is now on the right track.

However, they were not his assignment.

Acts 18: 4-7, 9-11.

In return for his concern, the Jewish people continually tried to kill him. In one instance, the disciples thought they had succeeded, *Acts 14: 19*. Apostle Paul finally got the point. He turned and started fulfilling the assignment that the Holy Spirit of Jesus had given him. He went to the gentiles. Thereafter, God assured him that he was on the right track.

In other words, when we take the Word of God to people who have not been set to *yet* hear it, there is no fruit, because the spirit of God's Word is not there. God's Word made sense as to why the discussion of His Word with each of these three women would always erupt in a vehement argument that started and ended with their use of the word, *but*.

For each one, the destruction of their lives started when they were children. Worse, the mother in each case was the impetus. One lady's personal hell has lasted for more than seven decades. Another, six decades. And the last one over five decades.

Every individual conversation with these ladies' meanders in and out through the past as though time has stood still. Any attempt to speak of their godly purpose was unable to break through the barricade of the past. And as such, they have been unable to tap into their divine *inbuilt* I.P.S. system.

Until the Holy Spirit of God opened my eyes, my behavior was the same. Now, I am able to look back and understand that the past was merely a temporary pit stop on the way to walking in my assignment for Jesus.

Nevertheless, change takes time. And sometimes, worldly love hinders God's work.

Chapter 5 Study Guide

1. The majority of most Christian congregations are women. Nevertheless, a multitude of women who profess to be Christians physically and verbally abuse their children.

   a. Why do you think this is happening?

2. God said in His Word that the teaching of *His* Word *will* bring everyone into the same unity of faith in Jesus and they will no longer be able to be kicked around by old habits and behaviors.

   a. Why do you think this is not happening?

Notes:

Chapter 6 – What's Love Got to do with it

Though it may look good, Loving anyone more than
Jesus is not of God, Matthew 10: 37, John 14: 21.

Three women, one man! Two of the three view the man's actions as though he personally set out to destroy their lives. The third was determined that she could save him. Each woman's life was negatively influenced and shaped by their involvement with him. A noteworthy point is that each woman grew up in church and yet became involved with a man who had not been raised knowing God.

When all was said and done, their lives looked like an A-bomb had been ignited. However, marriage had produced children. Thus, even though their relationships with him ended, those of the aunts, uncles, and cousins, etc. continued to mix.

One particular day started out with a conversation with one of his former wives. Strangely, the night ended with a second call, out of the blue, from another one. In both conversations, this man's behavior was the topic. What was surprising was the difference of opinions as to why he behaves as he does.

His penchant for choosing women who had a spirit of kindness and gentleness was known to the family. Who am I? A distant relative who was familiar with all parties.

The belief in God was the topic of our conversations, woman to woman. One had undergone a personal traumatic life-threatening event prior to meeting him. She was convinced that she was alive by the grace of God. Nevertheless, despite his horrendous treatment towards her, genuine love for him could be heard in her voice. On the other hand, another was convinced that he should know how to act.

Each lady had been impressed with his demeanor when they first met. He knew how to turn on the charm when necessary. In turn, they were convinced — by him — of his honest and sincere love.

He secretly met and married a third wife without anyone else knowing. And again, she professed faith in God. By this time, God had called me as a servant to His son Jesus.

Prayers were made that this time it would be different. It was hoped that this time, the love of Christ in her would make a difference in his life.

It didn't! Their relationship ended horribly.

Food is better when eaten in a house of love, love protects the true believer, love gives us hope,

All three survived but were emotionally scarred. His behavior did not just affect his wives. Children, family, and girlfriends, were also the recipient of his rage at life. All three wives asked what does love, or the lack of it, have to do with his ungodly actions.

Proverbs 15: 17; Romans 5: 5; Romans 8: 39.

"Everything, according to God," I replied.

None understood.

If not for the knowledge of the Word of God, the fact that three Christian women are unable to understand what the lack of *love* has to do with his behavior would be baffling. Two of the three feel that he *chooses* to hate. One thought she could *love him* out of hate.

According to scripture, no one *knowingly* chooses to hate, or the life that comes with rage. How do *I* know? *I was* where he is!

Damaged souls line the path of my rampage through life when I attempted life without God. And, I did *not* choose to be such a person. *We Are One* reveals why *godly love* is the key to freedom.

Surprisingly, the passage of years in the religious community indicates a sad truth. Many who are supposed to hold the key to the knowledge of *God's* way and *His Love*, have lost their way due to life. On the other hand, Jesus said the secular world has a better grasp of dealing with people as to the *cause and effect* of life.

God's Command: Men and women are to be taught how to love, **Titus 2: 2-4**

A few years back, a documentary was created on the malnourishment of love to infants and children. The results revealed that lack of love *altered* not only that child's ability to give love, *but to receive it.*

The secular world also seems to understand the concept of brainwashing. In one article, scientists took a ferocious fish and enclosed him in a *glass* tank within another tank. They filled the outer tank with the fish that the predator fish fed on. The fighter fish would charge the glass walls trying to get at his food. He couldn't. He eventually stopped. The inner tank was removed. Although the barrier was gone, the predator fish did not try to feed on its normal food that was now available. It had been brain-washed and changed from its *normal* inbred feeding habit.

It is written that Jesus said the world is wiser than the children of God because they understand how to deal with people, **Luke 16: 8.**

Lack of love is known to alter a child's behavior. Hence, Satan's attack on Eve in the Garden. It was all about *altering*

God's plan for dominating the world *through Love*. Disassociation from love can only produce hate.

The odd thing about facts is that they are never able to overcome *emotional devastation*. Intellectual truths cannot alter the reality of life.

The behavior of my mother, who hated her own child, was misunderstood until I met the master of her soul. This true story is revealed in my second book, *Purposely Unchained*.

The destruction of my soul was not the known target of my mother. She was merely the agent for the devil. Satan used her to put his bulls-eye on my divine purpose. Satan destroyed her life, and tried to wreck mine. But for God.

The secular world has gone to great lengths to brainwash the people to believe that true love is possible *without God*.

It is written that Jesus said *forgive them for they know not what they do*. Obviously, all involved knew they had betrayed Jesus, beat him, stabbed him and hung him on the cross. The consequence of their actions was looking at them from the cross, staring them in the face. Thus, Jesus was *not* talking about their *physical* actions. He meant they did not *spiritually* understand what they had done.

Yet today, Christians, as well as the secular world alike, blame the people for their inability to love. How can this be misunderstood given the *unchanging* truth of the Word of God?

Men and women react differently to the lack of love. Women cry out for help when love is lacking. And, we read an uncountable number of books about imaginary love. Men react with anger and abuse, and sometimes worse.

Personally, before God, the consequence of extensive reading about men who loved women forever, simply magnified that *I* was unlovable. As a woman, I tried all the ways suggested by the secular world in how to mold myself, on the *exterior*, of a person who was worth loving. I changed my walk, my talk, etc.

to try and please others. Sometimes, we will even accept abuse, physical and verbal, and call it love. None of my efforts, my remakes, worked because they were unable to influence the true problem.

No one had ever taught me to love myself as a wondrous and purposed creation of God. *We Are One* demonstrates that the person who had been given that command did not know it for herself. Thus, how could she pass it on?

Jesus said, teach the world by showing them what He has taught His people, His true church,

Matthew 28: 20.

We Are One demonstrates that this is not an abnormal occurrence between mothers and daughters. In fact, it is more common than not.

How do you help a loveless soul? It is not the love of man*kind*, for that love is fickle. Even the scriptures speak about it. Jesus supplied the solution. People have to *see* true love in action.

When our true God, creator of the Heavens and Earth, and mankind, Yahovah is his name, introduced Himself, His existence shook my world. It turned my life right side up as He began to reveal the reason for our actions. Of course, He started with mine.

Remember when your child had done something exceedingly exasperating and you picked them up and shook them. Not physically harming them, but letting them know enough is enough of their actions.

The result is in. What's love got to do with it? God said everything.

Back in the day, men would take a metal wrench and touch both the alternator and the battery on older cars at the same time to jumpstart a cold car. Eternal Love reached through time and did the same for me.

The Holy Spirit kick-started my *inbuilt* I.P.S. system into gear with a *Bruce Lee* spiritual kick to my mind. This event is recorded in my book: *Mine, an everlasting promise of Love*. However, cold engines take time to run smoothly.

When a soul has been so abused and hurt, and taught that it is worthless, human love cannot change that soul. Led by the Spirit of God, the past issues in my life were settled with my mother prior to her death. My relative did neither with his parents.

According to the scriptures, God says *all* souls belong to him. Thus, the *fixing* of a soul is only in God's hands, no matter how much another human loves you.

Separating ourselves from the Creator, and His *rules* of how to live, has consequences. We error, both men and women, by getting involved with people who do not know God.

The world that we live in today confirms the failures on a daily basis, as murder, robbery, rape, cheating, manipulation, conspiracy, etc. are daily headline news. Total disregard of human life is outlined daily in newspapers around the world.

On the other hand, God is not surprised. Christians should not be amazed. He told us in advance what would happen without Him. However, what should amaze us is that these same acts happen in the lives of professing Christians.

The question was, *What has love got to do with it?*

Everything.

The man in this story didn't choose to be unlovable. Living without love on a daily basis is cold. And, *it is frightening*.

What has love got to do with it? Everything, when it is the *love of God* that is missing. Only when *true love* steps into his life, will he know that he is somebody worthy of love. Then, he will be able to love in return.

The knowledge that God loves us teaches us to love ourselves. Then, we no longer act in perverse ways. *Then*, and only then, do we become able to love others. Then and only then can we *receive love*.

The mandatory laws of the U.S. suggest that the secular world understands the necessity for instruction in order to succeed in life. Moral teaching was at one time partially inclusive within this structured teaching to children. Then, the anti-Christ spirit went to great length to take prayer out of the schools.

The question must always arise. Could *Columbine*, and the school shootings since then, be the tip of *reaping* what Christians have sowed?

God alone quickens us, *makes us alive*, what formerly was dead.

What's Love Got To Do With It?

Everything!

Neither classes, nor television shows, can give life. They can only mimic a faint imitation of it. Only *true love* can touch what is *inwardly* dead, and make it come alive!

Who is *love?* Jesus is his name and there is no other name above that name.

While we wait patiently for *Love* to truly touch my relative, compassion is required, even though it may be like hugging a rose bush full of thorns. They will stab, cut and prick you, but once you get past the thorns, there is a beautiful flower.

What's Love Got To Do With It? Everything!

The following are eight things that Love does, and eight things that Love does *not* do.

Love is 1) long suffering, 2) kind, 3) bears all things, 4) trustful, 5) hopeful, 6) patient, 7) rejoices in triumph of truth, and 8) *never* fails.

On the other hand, Love never 1) is envious, 2) boastful, 3) conceited, 4) behaves unbecomingly, 5) self-seeking, 6) provoked, 7) or counts up wrongs and 8) rejoices at evil hurtful things.

This next story brings this truth home.

Chapter 6 Study Guide

1. God's unchanged design to proliferate mankind is through a husband and a wife. In addition, God left specific instructions about the qualities of a husband. Yet, women choose men who have no concept of God.

   a. Do you know anyone who did this?

   b. What do you think is the reason?

   c. Did the marriage last? Discuss.

2. God said the *man* is to look for a wife, not the other way around.

   a. What do you think is the reason women search for the man?

   b. Most importantly, have you seen the difference when God brings a man into a woman's life, and the opposite when the woman does the searching? Discuss.

Notes:

Chapter 7 – A Real Wonder Woman Dresses in God's Armor

The divine influence of Faith upon the heart, and its
reflection in one's life, is sufficient, for His power is
made complete in weakness, 2 Corinthians 12: 9.

William Moulton Marston created the character of Wonder Woman in 1941. Various interviews indicate that he had a very clear idea for the personality of his character. One particular article quotes him as stating:

"Wonder Woman is psychological propaganda for the new type of woman who should, I believe, rule the world," he said. "He further argued that the only hope for civilization is the greater freedom, development and equality of women in all fields of human activity."

Marston was right on target with God's creation of and the purpose of *the woman*. However, his lifestyle indicated that he lived outside the commandments of God. According to another interview, one of his wives suggested the female super wonder woman character. He had two wives.

A debilitating medical problem that cannot be healed is unimaginable for those of us who have not lived with such an issue. And yet, to maintain faith in Jesus in that situation seems to be beyond human strength. It is. But nothing is impossible for God.

The woman in the Bible with the issue of blood comes to mind. She maintained her faith in God for twelve years despite an illness that had left her bankrupt.

Mary Anne Cortus, Caucasian, maintained her faith and trust in God for 54 years, until the end. And, she affected everyone she met, no *infected* everyone, with a spirit of kindness and gentleness wherever she traveled.

Mary Anne exemplified the spirit of a real wonder woman in that she never gave in, nor bowed down, to the illness that had debilitated her life since childhood. Nor did she ever contemplate suicide. She knew her life was in the hands of God.

They, male *and female,* shall dominate and rule over the earth. She shall *help* the man bring My purpose of Love on earth to fruition, through teaching others to love.

Genesis 1: 26-28; 2: 18, 22;

Life did not just throw rocks at Mary Anne. It threw boulders at her, one after another. Nevertheless, Mary Anne chose to live with gusto.

God said in His Word that we are responsible for not only raising our own children, but teaching anyone else who is in our household. But, to fulfill this divine assignment, there has to be not only an intellectual knowledge of God, but a strange faith, i.e. total trust, in Him and the truthfulness of His spoken command over one's life.

Mary Anne and I first met over ten years ago at the Lutheran church that we both attended. Even then, she was on the verge of being wheelchair bound for the purpose of mobility. Nevertheless, each Sunday that she was able to attend, she would greet you with a smile. And, she was always ready with witty come-backs during Bible study discussions.

Back in the 50s and 60s, little girls grew up with the idea of being a super woman. Mary Anne's life exemplifies that of a true super hero.

She was diagnosed at the age of three with juvenile rheumatoid arthritis. Unable to truly pinpoint the disease, the doctors called it an auto immune blood disease, according to her husband. It was allegedly passed down genetically from her grandmother. While in college, she developed a thyroid condition that was derived from the autoimmune disease. The physician gave her what her husband calls "an atomic cocktail." It destroyed her thyroid gland. She required medication for the rest of her life. Later, she was diagnosed with Lupus.

She still did not quit.

Since childhood, Mary Anne's body had been under attack. Nevertheless, it did not stop her from living with gusto. Many may ask how? The Word of God answers.

Mary Anne was raised since childhood hearing about God. She grew up in the Lutheran faith. Her father was Episcopalian. Her father was the head of a church ministry. Therefore, Mary Anne heard about Jesus both at church and at home.

Parents are to teach their children and grandchildren the statutes and commandments of God because they prolong our life on earth,

The attack on her body led her to become a research biochemist with an MBA. She desired to be involved in clinical trial tests due to her illness.

Deuteronomv 6: 1-2. 5. 7:

Eventually she became employed by a company that produced medical plastics designed for the blood industry.

Her husband William Cortus said that she was a different scientist because she believed in God. William said she confessed to him one day that the deeper she delved into science, the more she could see the ultimate design of God. As the various illnesses progressed, she grew stronger. Her husband said she told the family that she believed that regardless of the disappointments in life, she still believed in the promise of her heavenly reward. And, the worse her condition became on earth, the greater her reward would be in heaven as long as she stayed faithful to God's truth.

The wonder woman spirit in Mary Anne held firm. However, I am getting ahead of the story. There were *hiccups* in her life prior to her journey with her husband William [Bill].

Like many women, regardless of their faith in God, she originally chose an ungodly man for a husband. She was warned. She ignored them. The price was high.

Her first husband did not want Mary Anne to take his last name. She retained her maiden name. When she became pregnant with her first child, which the doctors had said was impossible, he wanted her to have an abortion. In fact, based on her medical history, the doctors said she would never get pregnant. In their opinion, she was a two-percenter due to the destruction of her thyroid.

She refused to have an abortion. Mary Anne knew her pregnancy was a 100-percenter—if you will—from God. Time would prove this truth. Her first son would have an impact in her latter life that was unexpected.

Finally, her first husband left. Mary Anne decided that she would be a single parent for the rest of her life.

God had other plans for her. I understand.

Prior to my second husband and I getting married, we both had decided that we would never get married again. He had been married twice. I had been married once. God had other plans. We got married.

Abandonment by Mary Anne's first husband was a blessing. Due to her faith, she would not have left him. She would have stayed because of her faith in God's word about the importance of marriage.

God handled the problem. The door was opened for Bill and Mary Anne.

They met at a Toast Master event, in which people learn how to speak before a crowd. Bill was very involved in this organization. On the other hand, Mary Anne simply wanted to meet people who were single parents. She did not want to go to a bar or such. She chose the Toast Master group. After her 10th speech, Bill gifted Mary Anne with her award.

When they first met and started sharing their history, Bill was impressed.

"I had always wanted a wife who lived for Jesus Christ," he said.

Their love story was not without wrinkles. For a while, it was an on and off relationship before he knew that Mary Anne was the *wife* for whom he had been searching.

Marriage protects not only the husband and wife, but the children.

1 Corinthians 7: 13-14.

Bill said he had attended a men's conference. During one of the messages, he knew Mary Anne should be his wife. He invited her to the graduation ceremony. Afterwards, he asked her to marry him. However, due to his former hesitation, he had to convince Mary Anne that he would never leave her again. And, that he would be a faithful husband and loving father to her son.

He promised. He asked her again. She said yes. They were married in 1995.

Both Bill and Mary Anne decided at the beginning to stay faithful to their vows regardless of the turn of events. They did. He kept his promise to the end of her life.

Bill's father was a loud person who believed in corporal punishment where you would beat the nonsense out of children.

"I swore to myself that I would never be like my father," Bill stated during our interview.

Bill kept that promise both as a faithful husband and a loving father right up to the end.

After they married, Mary Anne continued to defy the medical declarations about her ability to be a mother. They had three more children. And, as parents, they made sure that all their children attended both Christian and regular schools and were taught about God and the truth of His Word. Today, all their children believe in Jesus.

Perhaps this is why the devil was intent in destroying Mary Anne since childhood. God knew she would stay faithful to His commands in both her marriage and family.

All of her children were miracle births because they were high risk due to her illness. Several years prior to her death, their youngest son got hit by a car. He almost died. He remained in a coma for a time. After regaining consciousness and recuperating, he became an assistant caregiver for his mother. His goal was to become her primary caretaker. He enrolled in school with that intent. However, Mary Anne died while he was in school. Nevertheless, he is dedicating his career to helping people like his mother.

A husband and wife are expected to remain faithful to each other that they may raise *godly* seed, children who know and love God,

Malachi 3: 15.

Mary Anne loved to travel. Bill's job allowed him to accumulate *reward* trips. He used them to take her wherever she wanted to go. She loved being out in the Red Wood Forest, the desert, Alaska, and the many other places where they traveled.

Sometimes she initiated the trip. More often, as time passed, it was Bill.

In addition, Mary Anne was a big sports fan. They attended many events right up to the end with the kindness of other people. Various equipment was needed to lift and transport her in and out of vehicles.

Despite her illness, Bill never regretted their marriage.

"I knew I had a divine purpose in her life, and she in mine," Bill stated. "We knew we were meant to be together."

Eventually, Mary Anne lost the ability to read. The numerous diseases had affected her eyesight. She still did not give up, especially on *hearing* the Word of God. Bill set it up for her to use a daily program called *Jesus Calling*. And, when she could no longer attend Sunday services, Bill would attend alone. Then he would go home and relate the message to Mary Anne.

"Our life was not perfect, but the love we shared made it possible to remain faithful," Bill said. "Her dedication to being independent and strong, and not clingy, made it possible for me to go out and do my work. And, through technology, I made sure that she could reach out to me."

"How did you do that?" I asked.

"I installed a tech doorbell at our house," Bill stated. When someone would ring the doorbell, it would ring my phone and I could see who it was and actually open the door."

True love has no boundaries as to what we will do for someone we love.

Mary Anne's illness had progressed to the point that she was almost one hundred percent dependent on others for her care. Bill decided to retire from his job to take care of her full time.

Given the various diseases that crippled her body, many people would have given up on life and God. What kept Mary Anne going?

The seed of Faith, that had been planted in the heart and soul of MaryAnne as a child, had grown to such proportions that it could not be up rooted by the travesties of life. Therefore, the more that the devil threw at her, the more reasons Mary Anne found to praise God.

Beatitudes, Matthew 5, 6, 7.

In simple terms, her *inbuilt* I.P.S. system kept her going. She knew God, thus she knew her value, her *identity*, as His child. She knew she had a *purpose* in this life outside the diseases that kept attacking her physical body. And, she knew and relied upon her faith in God, which was the *source of her strength.*

It is written, no commanded, by God in how we are to live. However, when even the minor details of His Word are ignored, or not known, the cost can be beyond our imagination.

The path of my personal life was permanently changed by an unexpected event.

Who was in charge? You decide.

Chapter 7 Study Guide

1. Faith was the foundation of Mary Anne's life regardless of the trials she endured because she was taught this truth from childhood.

   a. Do you think that knowing God's truth from childhood makes a difference in our faith walk?
      i. If not, Discuss.

2. Mary Anne's life was not without trials and a multitude of afflictions. Nevertheless, Mary Anne took God at His Word. Despite her personal illness, she was a *helper* through love to both her husband and her children.

   a. Do you know of someone whose journey was similar?

3. Do you think that her knowledge of God's Word was the key? Discuss.

Notes:

Chapter 8 – Faith is Not a Fast Food Item

Faith, which is first a gift, grows through the study
of the Word of God, John 17: 20; Ephesians 2: 8

She has dry gangrene, according to the record," one nurse whispered to a second one from across the room. "That's why it stinks so bad."

Their voices echoed across the stark white and gray cement walls until it reached my ears. The clarity of their comments was as though they were standing directly next to my hospital bed.

"What are you talking about," I asked.

Neither replied as they scurried out of the room like frightened mice running for cover. Their hasty exit made it obvious that they had spoken out of turn. But, in looking back, I am now convinced that God intended me to hear their words. Determined punches on the call button brought in a different nurse.

"Get the doctor in here now," I demanded.

While waiting, my thoughts meandered back to how I had arrived at this point. About eight weeks earlier, I had stepped onto a metal rim that was normally used to surround sinks to keep water from seeping beneath to the wood. It was lying outside in the yard during reconstruction in the house. After the accident, it became obvious that it was lying on top of something else. When I stepped on it, it reacted like a diving board that dips down with the weight of the diver and then pops back up with the weight gone.

It came down directly on my Achilles tendon at the back of my heel and completely severed muscles and tendon. The path that I had chosen for my life was forever altered by this accident.

After the initial surgery, it looked as though everything had healed, at least on the surface. Rehabilitation revealed the opposite.

Everything broke loose in the midst of therapy. The operating physician had been informed that the injury was caused by a piece of metal. Nevertheless, they failed to give me a tetanus booster. It opened the door for the infectious disease gangrene to take root and grow.

However, something else happened, which I believe saved my life. When the doctor came in and told me that I could lose my foot and possibly my leg, I blew up at him.

"You need to understand that I have things to do," I yelled. "I have just applied for entry into the Pro Bowlers organization for women. Thus, YOU need to do something about my foot."

Several doctors examined the wound. None agreed to operate. They were fearful of a malpractice suit for negligence. However, God had a *ram in the bush,* if you will. My family doctor knew an Osteopathic bone specialist. He recommended my case to him. He came. He didn't play.

"Yes, I can fix it, but it is going to leave an ugly scar," he stated.

"Will I be able to bowl?

"Don't you think you should be worrying about walking."

"I said, will I be able to bowl."

"Yes."

"Then schedule the operation."

At that time, osteopathic doctors had to have special permission to use the facilities at regular hospitals. Surgery required being moved to a different facility, for which I am very grateful. At one point after surgery, the use of an experimental drug was necessitated. The familiar antibody drugs were not having any effect on the infection. The new drug worked.

Today, ugly scar and all, I have two feet and the use of both legs. Thus, when Yahovah first opened my eyes to His existence, and I was complaining about the hardships of my life, He reminded me through His Holy Spirit that it was *Him* that had kept me during those years.

In looking back, I knew it was true.

In other words, I did not survive because of my stubbornness. The refusal to give in came from somewhere deep inside of my heart, soul, and spirit. It was this same spirit to survive that rose up when I shattered the same ankle years later.

It was approximately 6:30 a.m. Happy that Spring had arrived, the decision was made to go roller skating in an outside park several blocks from home. All was well until the wheels of one skate caught on a branch. The skate came to an abrupt stop. My body did not. POW. POW. The breaking of my ankle bones sounded like a 38-hand gun going off in my ear. When I came to my senses and looked down, my foot was turned almost upside down.

A foolish but lifesaving thought entered my mind. *I have really sprained my ankle.* A look around ascertained that I was at the back of the park, which was about half the size of a football field. No one would hear my call for help. I grabbed my foot with both hands and yanked it back into its proper position.

I blacked out from the pain.

Upon regaining consciousness, and using the pant leg of the *sprained* ankle, I lifted my left foot and laid it across the unbroken one. It was the same ankle where I had injured the Achilles tendon. From there, I scooted backwards until I was close enough to the front of the park. A group of men from the automobile sales store across the street ran over to assist. They called for an ambulance.

Friends asked did I think I was in a western movie. I could not answer as to the *source* of the urging to turn my foot. However, the ambulance driver said my action kept blood flowing to my foot. God in control.

The source of my determination was unknown until I read God's Word. It was God. This *source of* strength had sustained me in many other instances.

The point is that *until* God opened my eyes to His truth, I was unaware that it was Him all the time, and Him *in me*, that had been keeping me alive. Prior to this, I believed that it was my determination because I believed that I knew who I was, my strength, and my set purpose.

It wasn't. It was all God. Thus, informing people that they can choose God and Faith, as though they are items on a fast food menu, is completely in opposition to the Word of God.

Wounds often grow a scab that make it look as though it is healed. But, sometimes, it is a rotting mess beneath the surface.

People *look* as though they are healed from life. Time proves they are not.

God alone calls us in and puts us into the body of His Son Jesus. Until then, no one can come to Jesus,

John 6: 44, 65.

Individuals go to work. They attend games afterwards. Teenagers go to school. Everything *looks* normal until it isn't. Men killing wives and families, women killing children, boyfriends killing girlfriends, etc., clearly demonstrate that *spiritual* gangrene is the same as in the natural. And, it spreads.

Hurt people hurt people.

The subtlety of this pattern, and how I had unwittingly carried it forth at one time, was a horrifying thought. Through the age-old trickery of the devil, I had become what I hated. If not for God and the truth of His Word, Satan would have used my awareness of my errors to keep me in bondage to him through guilt.

The Armor of God is *spiritual* battle gear for our minds and souls. Our *inbuilt* I.P.S. system helps us to wear it properly. And, when we are dressed correctly, the journey from bondage to freedom is guaranteed.

Jesus SAID although there will be afflictions and anguish in the world, Believers in Him will yet have *inner* peace because He has conquered the world, i.e. the enemy,

A disturbing fact yet abounds in today's world of religion. Many professing Christians believe and teach that talking about Satan is

John 16: 33.

giving the devil honor. And, that it is out of God's will.

This erroneous concept begs the question to be considered. Is God giving Satan honor since He is the *first* to tell believers about this enemy? More so, *We Are One* reveals a divine truth about this adversary. It will change the life of every woman, no matter the age. This truth is the *missing* ingredient that has been hidden away from women for centuries.

The Woman has a *divine* command to teach others, sons and daughters, how to *truly* love first God, then self, then others with a sound mind, i.e. one that is based on faith in Jesus, **Matthew 22: 37; Philippians 2: 1-2; Titus 2: 3-4.**

Satan's methodology must be exposed where it can be understood. If we don't, we will always be in bondage, never delivered, never free, and always repeating the past.

Through the influence of Satan, religious and non-religious people plotted and planned to kill Jesus. Period. The Jewish nation rejected even the possibility that Jesus was the promised Messiah.

What are we doing today? We name it. We claim it. And then what? The world is steadily dissolving in hate.

Our mission is eternal. You, the woman, are God's appointed transformer for a special assignment. You, the woman, are His divine helper. And You, the woman, are the only one that has this assignment. This commandment about our true purpose has been hidden and buried for centuries. It is the reason why we, the Women, are the target of the devil.

This *deliberate* ploy by the enemy has left an uncountable number of women struggling through life. It can be likened to being trapped in the mud at the bottom of the ocean while reaching for the distant glitter of sunlight on the water's surface. Sometimes, the woman drowns.

Throughout the Bible, God changed the names of people to indicate their true purpose for Him. In certain countries, the village helped name the child. Since then, people started naming their children after animals, trees, etc. Today, many names have no meaning because they are merely a group of letters thrown together. Sometimes, the children can barely pronounce their given names.

What does your name say about you? God has a way of surprising us even in something as supposedly minor as our names. It may surprise you. Having grown up with the demonic concept of my personal worthlessness, the meaning of my name was stunning, but yet enlightening.

My name Muriel, in Irish, means sun light, or sun bright shining on the water. However, in Hebrew, it means *the flame of God. Uriel,* [Anglicized from the Hebrew] was the name of a man chosen by King David to carry the Ark of God, and to minister to Yahovah *forever.*

For me, the *flame, and/or light* of God, was demonstrated since childhood by a *smile from within*. Satan knew what it meant. Thus, he tried to *snuff* out my inner light through abuse. Sadly, my mother was his instrument. Regardless, the devil failed.

Today I am a servant to God and His Son Jesus. And my smile is yet intact.

Hearing people proclaim, albeit sincerely, that people choose to serve Satan is still surprising. Even as recently as this Spring, a discussion was had with a person who said he had grown up in church. Nevertheless, he could not imagine that people truly did not believe that God existed.

We met in a place of business. And, as I am oft to do, the subject of Faith and God arose. During the revelation of my former life as an atheist, he admitted that he could not conceive such a truth, even though it is contained in God's Word. His next question was not unexpected.

"What did I think about the trees, flowers, etc. and their origin?" he asked.

Over the past twenty-four years, the same question has been repeated often by perplexed Christians. The scripture they always refer to is *Romans 1: 20* that states that the visible things [in life] show the invisible power of God. However, people seldom include verses 16-19, and 21-25. These verses clearly state that Apostle Paul is referring to people that *previously knew* the righteous of God. Verse 21 is clear. It states that when the people *knew* God, they were not thankful, etc. In other words, these scriptures in totality are speaking to people who *used to know* God, rather than those who *never* knew God.

In other words, the Bible is written for believers and *not* non-believers.

God left us the truth in His Word. In my past life, since God did not exist, and neither did Satan, why would I choose either?

One chooses eggs or waffles because by experience a person has tasted both. Therefore, they have the ability to decide between the two. A choice is made for one or the other, or both, due to like or dislike. However, if one does not know, or has experienced God, how can one select either to serve God, or Satan?

In *We Are One*, the stories of several women portray the difference in their lives by *choosing* Yahovah, our heavenly Father and His Son Jesus. How? Through the power of their *inbuilt* I.P.S. system. Despite the circumstances that tried to derail them, it always guided them back to God out of the darkness of despair.

The study of His word revealed that although I was in the world, in plain sight, I was *spiritually* hidden. My awakening made me an exposed target for Satan.

Was I ready? Absolutely, or God would not have called me in. Now I am able to say yes although not in the beginning. It was time to grow up through a specialized training course that was designed by God. The details are included in my book *Purposely Unchained.*

A man had a son possessed by a demon, as did a woman's daughter. Jesus rebuked the demons and delivered both out of the control of the demon.
Matthew 15: 22, 28; 17: 15, 18.

On the other hand, *We Are One* also illustrates the stories of a few women who could not overcome the pitfalls of life.

The world's successful campaigning of Satan as a cartoon character would be humorous if it were not so injurious to Christians. In biblical times, the people *knew* that evil spirits possessed people and *spiritually* influenced them to destroy themselves, and others.

When Apostle Peter attempts to stop, deter, and alter the purpose for which Jesus came to earth, Jesus speaks to the spirit functioning from within Peter and identifies it as the spirit of Satan.

Plainly, Jesus speaks aloud into the ears of Peter. But He is addressing the demonic spirit that is in Peter. Later scriptures indicate that Peter was unaware that he was an instrument for Satan, which was revealed when he denied knowing Jesus.

Satan does not have horns, a tail and wear a red cape. Scripture makes it clear that the devil is a wicked fallen angel, who is a spirit, that uses humans to achieve his purpose.

Who are the devil's helpers? There is no specific nationality, origin, dress code, head wrap, nor size or shape that identifies the ministers of Satan.

Who are they? Anyone and everybody that interferes with and tries to derail your destined purpose. In one incident, Satan's minister presented himself as my human angel of mercy. Nevertheless, God used it for good, to change my physical location.

Initially, the loss of everything that I owned was perceived as a nightmare. Time would reveal that God was moving me into position for the next level of my assignment.

Chapter 8 Study Guide

1. In this chapter, God was faithful to His Word and shows that even before I knew of His existence, He was aware of mine, and was looking out for me.

    a. Have you or someone you know experienced His love and faithfulness, even before they knew it was God looking out for them?

    b. Do you believe this is so?

    c. If not, discuss.

Notes:

Chapter 9 – A Judas Kiss Led to Freedom

Do not take vengeance on wrongdoers. Wait on the Lord
for He will avenge His people, Proverbs 20:22

T he fast-paced click, click, click, of women's shoes on the concrete floor announced women rushing in to find the expected bargain, or two. However, his casual saunter into the swap meet was slow and methodical. Men usually take their time because they don't want to be targeted as prospective clients.

After several minutes, he approached me with a stunning offer of help.

All offers of help are not from God.

"I've heard of your problems," he stated. "I believe I have the solution. I have a building over on Crooked Path road. You can store your items in my building."

2 Corinthians 11: 13-15

His words were music to my ears. It seemed that God had answered my prayers. The judicial decision had allowed for only a few days to vacate the premises.

"Then you must also be aware that I have no money to pay rent?" I responded.

"I am not looking for rent." He said. "However, if you use my location as a selling point for the vendors, it will generate customers to my business."

He explained his business. His offer was accepted.

It didn't take long to discover that this offer of help was not from God. The first indication that there was trouble in paradise came from a visit by the city officials of the township where his building was located.

"Is Mr. James in?"

"No, he isn't. Can I help you?"

"We noticed the sale this past weekend at his building," he stated. "Are you aware that his license to operate has expired?

"No, I was not."

"Before reopening the doors for business, please have him contact us immediately."

Rising anger tried to rear its head. A hard swallow kept it down.

"What needs to be done?"

"First, his license has to be renewed," the official stated.

When my angel of mercy returned, a demand for an explanation merely led to more excuses as to why he had left this information out of our original conversation. His justification was normal when people are caught in a lie. He simply created and manipulated more facts.

"I really thought I was helping you." he calmly stated without even a twitch.

"Did you know your license was expired?"

"Yes."

"And you didn't think it was important for me to know this fact."

"I thought you would have time to find a permanent location before the city approached you."

It had only been a week.

Television shows and movies always promote characters that are able to read people's mind. It's a good thing that Mr. James could not perceive my thoughts. Gritting my teeth to keep my former manner of behavior from exploding, a date was set to renew his license—at my expense.

It was not the first time that I had fallen prey to a predator. One would think that I had learned the lesson of depending only on God. I thought I had. The eventual loss of money and merchandise revealed the opposite.

Life seen in hindsight has a way of putting scriptural truths into proper perspective whether we like it or not. Satan used words to trick Eve. She then shared *those same words* with Adam. This so-called angel of mercy used words to speak an offer of *false help* into my ears with the sole purpose of self-benefit.

Compassion for others and forgiveness has great benefits. Refusal to forgive has serious consequences.

Matthew 18: 22-35

In the end, in addition to handling the cost of his license and permits, money was borrowed *under false pretensions* with the promise of repayment. It wasn't. But then events really took a strange twist.

When I prepared to sue him, the Holy Spirit reminded me how much I had been forgiven, which was a great deal more. The registered letters of demand went into the trash can. God would handle him.

Familiarity with cheating and lying in the world was one thing. In the world of religion, it was not expected—that is until I studied God's Word. Mr. James had presented himself as a Christian.

We are *created by God* to be hooked to another. Since Satan is very aware of the imparted divine order of existence, he makes sure that we continually match up with ungodly people. It is how he keeps us angry. But it is up to the *body of Christ* to know and understand the *wisdom* of God's Word as it relates to our place in the world.

According to several biblical stories, the inspiration to move towards our godly purpose sometimes requires a Judas kiss.

The multiple acts of disloyalty by a professing Christian were exposed in a courtroom. In contrast to my worldly upbringing, they had grown up in church hearing about God. The case was lost twice. Once in regular court and then at the appeal level. It was a blessing.

If not for the deceit, and the biased judicial decision, retaining the building would have kept me in hock to an ungodly land owner. The result would have been extreme debt along with financially struggling to maintain and operate a building on a shoe-string budget. Instead, the acts of betrayal opened the door to liberty and sent me forward on my destined path.

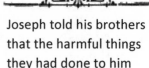

Joseph told his brothers that the harmful things they had done to him were used by God to save much people alive.

Genesis 50: 20

However, this wisdom came later. At first, the unjust decision was merely a stumbling block. The battle ceased only when all help from people, all appeals, and a total lack of financial help was exhausted. Suddenly, my spiritual place of habitation was an abandoned island — except for the presence of God.

God simply waited on me to arrive at this place of understanding.

Losing any fight is bad. But, defeat in a battle where you believe God was on your side has a strange secondary effect. The devil will have the people of God to believe that when life's ventures fail, it is God, and thus His Word that failed.

The devil is a liar.

The opposite is true. When all else fails, we have to rely upon our *inbuilt* I.P.S. system, which came from God.

In the beginning, during our creation, Yahovah, our heavenly Father, instilled into us our spiritual D.N.A., our *identity* as His pre-ordained creation in love, and our destined *purpose*. Then, by the blood of Jesus, a formidable, unbreakable, source of *strength*, by Faith in Him, is instilled in His re-born children.

Testing, persecution, make it surge to the surface, like butter from churned milk.

The Holy Spirit trains us until we are the image of Jesus Christ and able to present this wondrous truth to those who are still lost in bondage. The world is waiting for the *Sons of God* to appear. Who are they? Every person that God has called and put into the body of Christ.

Ephesians 1: 4-5 Romans 8: 18-21; John 6: 44, 65.

Errors, trials, and tribulations, are stumbling blocks. The first disciples kept tripping and falling until they understood. Scriptures are stairsteps to get us back on the right path.

One of the side effects of being betrayed is that the person who has been hurt tends to put that characteristic *of abandonment on* God. I did.

JESUS SAID His people are to teach the Gospel to the world by teaching them to watch the behavior of His True believers.

Matthew 28:19-20

It is also written to not let the sun go down and still be angry. I did. It is also written that we are not to give the devil a place to occupy in our lives, i.e. our minds. I did both. In fact, I opened the door so wide — through rage and anger — that the devil and his whole entourage — so it seemed — waltzed up into my house.

God was not pleased with my behavior. The visitors from hell, by God's approval, reminded me of a few truths. My I.P.S.

system kicked into high gear, neck roll attitude and all. You know what I'm talking about ladies.

When the business owner had walked into the market, the *spirit of desperation* was probably flashing above my head like a neon light. Thus, the owner's offer had truly seemed like an answer from God. However, the cost was greater than I could have imagined. On the other hand, this debacle was not about the business owner. It was about my destined journey for God as the servant of Jesus.

God's word would indicate that I was at fault.

When I whined to God about why He had not warned me before I committed the error. He replied *I did.* How? He sent me to His Word. It contained more than one caution.

After everything had fallen apart, the Holy Spirit used a dream to counsel me about the uselessness of trying to deter people from a path they are determined to take.

In the dream, I broke free from where I had been locked up to keep from cautioning people about a business they were about to embark upon. The people in the dream ignored my warnings and went into business with others who eventually caused them harm. This was one of my *Duh, Muriel* moments.

This dream took place about four years after the judicial case ended. God was telling me that even if He had sent people to warn me, I would not have believed them and would have found a way to do it anyway.

This venture, as a whole, started with me trying to help someone else realize their dream of being in business. However, their duplicity simply exposed the true spirit that was in them from the beginning. I didn't see it. But God did.

Regardless, each and every person must be forgiven as Jesus directed. Grudges cannot be held because people truly do not understand what they are doing. This truth was brought to my attention by yet another Judas kiss.

Several years later, I thought I had my former behavior — of striking back at people — under control as a reformed Son of God. Treachery against me exposed the truth. A darn root *of revenge* was still buried in my soul.

A letter was utilized to express the full extent of my rage about yet another Judas betrayal. God was not pleased with my behavior. In turn, the Holy Spirit used a manner of correction that even today causes an ache in my heart and soul at my failure.

The pastor was teaching about not whining about the events in life that challenge our faith. He used the story of Daniel in the sixth chapter as an example of perseverance in the face of tribulation.

A synopsis of his story is simple. The head Governors, princes, etc. of the king did not like Daniel. They set a trap to trip him up in his faith. They convinced the king to make a special decree. Anyone thereafter who would ask Yahovah God for help rather than the king would be fed to the lions. The king signed the Royal statute. He did not know this was against Daniel. He liked Daniel.

Daniel did not change his behavior or his prayer life. Scripture states that when Daniel knew the decree had been signed, he went home and prayed to Yahovah before an open window. Of course, his enemies were spying and listening. They reported him to the king, who was obligated to follow through with the specifics of his decree. Nevertheless, scripture reveals that God was in control.

The point that the pastor was making was that at no time did Daniel run to the king and whine and complain about his enemies. Nor did he confront those who had betrayed him to the king. The pastor also brought out the fact that Daniel was a senior citizen at this time, rather than the erroneous pictorial depictions where he was still a young boy. Also, the pastor stated that Daniel's faith did not just occur. His faith had been growing since he was a teenager, if not before.

The pastor asked the congregation how would our faith stand such a test. He wasn't asking about being thrown in the lion's den. He was inquiring how would our faith stand up in lieu of confronting our enemies, and or reporting them to the heads of corporations.

The pastor used Matthew 16, versus 24 through 25, to finish the message where Jesus teaches his followers to pick up their cross and follow him. More so, whosoever will save his own life will yet lose it. In the midst of this sermon, the Holy Spirit used this message to give me a spiritual whipping. It was yet by the word.

Instead of Matthew 16, I *heard* Matthew 5: 44-46, and immediately started bawling like a baby. Of course, these were familiar verses in which Jesus makes it clear how we are to treat our enemies.

My sheep, i.e. my followers, i.e. those who believe and trust in me, will have eternal life. And no one, nor thing, can snatch them out of our authority, because the Father and I are One.

John 10: 27-30

Sunday messages were always available online at this church without charge by Tuesday morning. After listening to the message twice, the realization of what had happened left me in tears again.

Matthew five was not part of the pastor's message. But, the intent of the Holy Spirit was clear. The Holy Spirit had reminded me that I had failed to *love* my enemy.

My reaction to the Judas kiss was not that of a *spiritual* Son of God. Worse, if at any time this person and I ever met again, I would be unable to exchange through communication the love of Christ. This spiritual spanking brought to mind why this was a familiar reaction. Believe it or not, it had to do with the past.

Rejection by a parent from childhood, followed by rejection by a husband, followed by rejection by friends, who all professed to love me but acted to the contrary, had left a hidden root of anger in my soul. The exposure by God of the hidden trap gave me freedom. In a nutshell, my reaction was the same spirit that had been in my mother.

I had been infected with a *spiritual* H.I.V. virus of hate, which the devil had planted in my mother's soul which originated from the pain of rejection.

In other words, a synopsis of our thoughts was *how dare you not like me?* After all, we changed how we talked, how we walked, and how we dressed. We tried to help everyone who asked. Nothing worked.

Changing for God by God works.

The absence of love, and or the violation of her love, negatively changed my mother's life forever. By the grace of God, and the gift of a husband from God, who loved me unconditionally, Love permanently changed my life for the good.

Satan is good at his job. However, he cannot out do Yahovah, our heavenly Father and God. Nor can the devil remove us out of the authority of our Lord and Savior of our Salvation, Jesus Christ.

Jesus said he came to give us freedom. That settles it. By faith in him we are free. There is nothing the devil can do about it.

Still, Satan does not give up? He gets Christians to put on costumes.

Chapter 9 Study Guide

1. The world begins teaching children in prenursery that getting other people to like you is being a good boy or girl. On the other hand, the Word of God teaches that *first* we are to love God first, ourselves second, and THEN the neighbor.

    a. Why do you think the world turned this around?

    b. If God's command were followed, do you think there would be less hatred?

    c. If yes, discuss why?

    d. If not, discuss why.

2. God says trust only Him. Mankind continually promotes that people can be trusted.

    a. Could this be why children are taught to trust people?

    b. Is the world deliberately creating prey for the predators?

    c. Could the world's teaching of *trust* people be as simple as making *habit* stronger than the Word of God?

        i.   Discuss.

Notes:

Chapter 10 – Take Off the Ostrich Feathers

God is looking for those who will worship Him in spirit and in truth,
John 4: 23-24.

Satan's presence and influence is clearly depicted throughout the scriptures. God's word also clarifies the fact that Satan can cause Christians to doubt God's Omnipotence, His love and the truth of His promises. Thus, God developed a unique method to invalidate Satan's tricks.

He created the concept of show and tell, but with a twist.

Starting with creation as a whole, stuff happened. Along the way, He parted a sea, changed rods into serpents, and made the sound of the footsteps of four lepers sound like a full army of marching men with horses and chariots. These are just a few examples. In each instance however, the telling preceded the showing.

In Ezekiel 37, He takes the prophet to a valley full of bones where He asks Ezekiel, "Can these bones live?" Since God does not ask questions just for conversation, it would seem that He was checking out two things. One, did the prophet believe in the perpetuity of God's promises, and two, did Ezekiel really believe that God's omnipotence surpassed the finality of death.

Ezekiel wisely answered that only the Lord God knew.

God then commands him to tell the bones to *hear* the word of the Lord. What follows is stunning proof of God's supremacy and therein lies the hope for all believers as to the irrevocability of God's promises.

According to what is written—for our benefit—the bones loudly come together and are made alive. However, the next sequence in events is a harsh reminder of the effect of flesh.

The scriptures state that the bones have been dry and dead for a long time. However, the first thing they do upon coming alive is to find fault with God. Their complaint is that they no longer have hope. In other words, in their opinion, their death provided the fodder for their loss of faith in God's promises.

Despite their attitude, God's mercy prevails. This *tell and show* episode served the purpose of showing the house of Israel that God's promises are infinite. Likewise, it is a reminder of the preeminence of God's word and His promises for today's believers on two levels.

Yahovah had Aaron throw down a rod that became a serpent. The Pharaoh's magicians and sorcerers of Satan did the same. Aaron's serpents swallowed *all* the serpents of Satan's people, **Exodus 7: 10-12.**

First, with the calling forth of sinews and flesh to the dry bones, Christians are given a Birdseye view of the ingenuity of God's handiwork in the creation of mankind. These specifics are not included in the first or second chapters of Genesis. Secondly, Christians can see that death does not nullify His promises.

But, as always, Satan tries to duplicate what God does. Scripture reveals the outcome. It was not good, at least for the devil.

War, disasters, senseless acts of perversity, and death itself, always brings forth the timeless question, "Where was God?"

The writings of Ezekiel demonstrate that God has not moved nor changed. And, *Hebrews 6: 11* reminds the followers of Jesus to remain industrious and fully confident in God's promises and full of hope to the end. God's *tell and show* production to Ezekiel is just one example of His continuing love and mercy. He showed the prophet that He had not given false hope to the Israelites. The life, death, and resurrection of Jesus Christ confirms that the promises to His other sheep are also true.

Therefore, regardless of the circumstances, the earthly body of Christ must place our trust, thus our hope, in Jesus Christ along with obedience to His commands. Therein is the only path of hope eternal. *Matthew 19:16-17.*

God wrote us a letter—the Holy Scrolls. In it, He had His truth recorded for our benefit. It gives detailed storylines of love and hate, obedience and disobedience. And, most importantly, He shows us the consequences of both sides of the coin, if you will.

Now, and especially in the end, Jesus will have nothing to do with darkness because He is light. And darkness and light cannot coincide in the same space. This truth is expressed even in the natural. Regardless of how dark a room is, a small, single match, chases the dark away.

However, God also left numerous warnings that we could foresee the consequences of our behavior. Nevertheless, the world of religion has seemingly, if not deliberately, decided that God's people do not need to know the fullness of this information.

This is not said in jest.

At one particular bible study some time ago, a new member in the congregation directed a question to me about Satan. Before I could complete my response, the pastor literally repeated the actions of the minister who had metamorphosed into a spiritual Darth Vader when I was a teenager.

Psalms 33: 11;

Isaiah 46: 10.

He stood up and towered over the new member. He demanded that I cease from talking about Satan. Albeit furious with his level of blindness, I adhered to his desire until bible study was over.

During our follow-up verbal conversation, I demanded to know why he wanted his female member to remain ignorant of Satan's devices. Especially in that she had acknowledged in tears that Satan was destroying her life, according to her testimony. She was so terrified that even in our midst, her entire body was shivering and quaking.

His unholy explanation was that talking about Satan was giving the devil too much credit. I reminded him of the scriptures where God warned us about Satan, over and over. I then asked him, "Are you wiser than God?"

Of course, he had no answer.

Through Satan's influence, nonbelievers in God and Jesus, have created one of the best marketing programs in the world. Satan is a cartoon character who wears tights, a red cape, and carries a pitchfork. This lie, successful for centuries and right up to today, is right up there with the promoted lie that Jesus' life, death and resurrection, has something to do with chocolate candy, chicken eggs and rabbits.

On the other hand, these two erroneous concepts have produced economic benefits for the world beyond imagination.

For people like myself, who denied the very existence of God, the depicture of Satan was humorous. That is until I met the *real* McCoy. Now we have movies and television shows perpetrating Satan and his various followers as saviors of the world.

Was there an uproar by the religious community as a whole? No!

God never left us in the dark about Satan's existence. Numerous scriptures, starting with Genesis and ending with Revelation, warn us about Satan and his goals. How much more explicit could God have made his warning?

Yet, various religions *refuse* to teach God's truth about Satan. In other words, his methodology, how he gets people to offend God, is not taught, despite the fact that God himself did not leave it a mystery. This religious cowering with the head-in-the-sand ostrich position leaves Satan running rampart around the world, including God's people.

My mother, as her pastor said when I went to him for help, was described as a good, tithe paying, woman. Never mind the fact that Satan was in full control of her life. She was a member of this one church for 60 years.

The devil destroyed her life. On the other hand, he left her alive and breathing while sitting on a church pew.

Lack of knowledge of this enemy left me wide open to attack. If not for God, I would still be running—in the opposite direction—away from Him.

Remember how your parents would grab you by your shirt, or ear, to stop you from doing certain things. I often tell people that God—the Father—spiritually grabbed his child by the collar through his Holy Spirit.

In the book of Job, God allows us to see that although He alone knows our *whole* heart, Satan also knows us, particularly our weaknesses.

Satan *knew* many things about me, and none of them were good. Satan knew I didn't understand death. Up to that point, no one that I *loved* had ever died. He was also aware that I knew nothing about God although my mother was a member of a church for 60 years. And he knew I loved wicked, evil movies about monsters.

About a week after my second husband's family had left for home after his funeral, Satan made his formal appearance in the form of my husband. Yes, I intellectually *knew* William was dead, but my grief and loneliness wanted him back.

I was not sleep when he came. In fact, I was wide awake because I was having a difficult time sleeping after Doug's death. Overwhelming grief led me to accept that it was my beloved. Why? *Religious people* were always talking about loved ones coming back.

Lying there in the dark, I felt the bed move as though Doug were getting in bed as he usually did. He always got behind me and then would pull me to him, protecting me in my sleep as he did when we were awake. Everything about the feel of this body felt exactly right. His body cupped mine as usual.

Doug had stood 6'2." In his youth, he had played semi-professional football. The muscles in his arms were like steel. His sinewy thighs had always required a larger size pant. The waist would then be tailored to fit his smaller waist.

It was his arms encircling me. His muscular thighs felt familiar. However, when I turned my head to look into his eyes, *it* would not allow me to turn. The harder I struggled, the tighter *it* held me, locking me in place.

Suffocating fear took over. I began biting at the arms as I screamed. No sound filled the room. In the midst of this intense struggle, a memory of what I often heard during church services came to mind.

"In the name of Jesus," I began, but I couldn't remember anything else.

I just started screaming — in my mind — the name Jesus, over and over.

The next thing I remember is waking up the next morning. The recollection of what had happened was gone. That is until I knelt to pray.

The memory flooded my consciousness, like a Tsunami coming on shore. I jumped to my feet crying out. I called the only person I knew who could tell me what happened.

It is a good thing to have a Christian mentor that will lead you to God's Word.

She also reminded me of another biblical promise.

"The power of the name of Jesus is greater than any name or any *demonic* power," she said. "That is why you peacefully went to sleep."

In a nutshell, I had just experienced Satan's determination to keep and control what he obviously believed belonged to him.

Me!

After all, I had spent my lifetime serving the spiritual wickedness of Satan through serving mankind.

Did I yet really understand what had happened?

No!

Why?

Again! Most religious services do *not* teach about how to live holy in spite of Satan's tactics. Many would argue otherwise. But, if this were so, then Satan would not be running rampart through the lives of professing Christians.

Discussions over the years with a multitude of the people of God clearly indicate that they have good intentions. But by the end of the day, many have *not* changed from the former deeds of their *old* man. Then, guilt sets in.

However, God never tells us to do what is impossible. Thus, there is a way to be renewed and changed in how we think about life with Jesus and our part in His kingdom.

In short, God made mankind in His image and likeness. He left instructions that we wouldn't get lost. The directives were ignored and a rescue plan was implemented. However, while lost, we picked up some really bad attitudes and behaviors, thus the command in Ephesians 4:22-24.

It states that Christians are to take off the old man and put on the new man. In plain English, remove the stinkin' thinkin' and replace them with honorable thoughts. God said this will result in righteous actions. This sounds simple enough, almost like changing clothes. Yet, in many cases, the adherence to this scripture is as elusive as the proverbial pot of gold. However, God does not issue unattainable commands. Therefore, He also provided a solution.

We, disciples [learners] are to bear fruit, but not from our own efforts doing it our way. Jesus tells us how in His Word.

In that believers are God's building in the making, let's start by taking a look at how a wood and brick house is erected.

In every instance without fail, the ground requires cleanup and leveling. Only then does construction begin. During the process, crews check for cracks on a daily basis. Without this care for detail, seemingly unimportant small fissures could worsen until the structure becomes unstable. Spiritual construction should be no different.

First, view the scriptures as God's tools.

The hard biting truth of His Word is the heavy-duty excavator. It removes the embedded stones and thorns left in the ground of the heart by the former tenant, the Adversary. Once the foundation (i.e. Jesus) is laid, the gospel becomes the nails, screws, and adhesive for the frame. In the natural, insulation is required prior to siding or roofing.

God's love for us performs this service.

This second step is an essential part of the solution because the devil will try to undermine and shake the foundations of your faith. From scripture, and up to today, he starts his plan of destruction when we are children.

Better yet, when the house is built on the shifting sand of *fake* belief, the devil knows all he has to do is send a flood, or two. From the astounding details of this next story, he sent a Tsunami to wash this woman away.

He thought he succeeded. He didn't.

Chapter 10 Study Guide

1. People are very grateful to be saved.

    a. However, have you experienced those who complain of life at every turn?

        i. Why do you think this happens?

    b. Do they know that the devil is the source of wickedness and unrest in our souls and spirit?

    c. Do they know that they are in a battle between good and evil?

2. Religiosity often claims it is simply people in the flesh, and don't want to change.

    a. What do you think?

3. Could it be that no one is explaining to them that naming and claiming Faith is not walking *in* faith?

Notes:

Chapter 11 – A Determined Queen Lives

Sometimes the journey to check out the truth
of the knowledge of God is long, 1 King, 10:1.

The world marvels when stories arise of people who survived unthinkable circumstances. They wonder what made that person keep getting up and fighting, regardless of how often they were knocked down. This concept of *guts and glory* is not new.

The Bible is full of stories about people who survived impossible situations. But, they did more than endure. They emerged stronger and more determined than ever before to survive.

Apostle Paul comes to mind. At one point, he was beaten to the extent that the other disciples thought he was dead. However, his godly assignment was not completed. It is written that Paul revived. More so, he went back into the same town from which the men had come who had beaten him. Then there are the young men who refused to worship an idol. They were thrown into a furnace that was so hot it burned up their captors. The young men escaped unharmed.

In each of the biblical stories, the devil had an agenda to destroy them. He failed. He thought to destroy Makeda. He failed.

Makeda had a purpose. Therefore, nothing that the devil threw at her could deter her from the purpose and mission that

God had created and assigned to her. Nevertheless, the devil threw everything but the kitchen sink at her in the attempt to destroy her before she could achieve her divine assignment.

Satan's plan did not work. But he made her life very difficult.

Due to the circumstances surrounding her birth, Makeda's mother did the unthinkable. She allowed men to use her child as a sex toy. But I'm getting ahead of the story.

Makeda, born in 1971, whose birth father was Creole, grew up in church. Her grandfather was a minister. Her grandmother was on the board of the southern Baptist church. Nonetheless, life would not be easy.

Makeda adored her mother. Nonetheless, the woman who gave birth to her continually rejected her because she was the daughter of a man who was no longer in the mother's life. Male family and friends were allowed to rape and molest Makeda as a child. Initially, she was taken to the doctor because of her complaints about sexual abuse. The mother insisted that she had not been raped.

There were never repercussions for the boys. In fact, the stepfather had molested Makeda. Her mother insisted that she had made a fraudulent charge because she wanted her real dad. A male cousin molested her when she was seven years old. She was passed around like a sex toy among the male members of her family. Eventually, she became sexually promiscuous.

"I knew how to have sex better than many grown women," Makeda said. "One cousin would give me sex books and tell me to choose the position to use when they had sex."

The thought was instilled in her mind that being used for sex was her purpose in life because she also became aroused. It would be years before she realized the perfection of the human body as created by God. In other words, our sexual organs are intended to cause arousal for the purpose of intimacy with our husbands. Eventually Makeda began to call men *penis people*. Between 1987 to 1989, life became more difficult.

Her grandmother died.

By this time, Makeda had gotten involved in a relationship with a young man whom she really liked. She would soon discover that they were related. The knowledge of his identity came about by accident.

Makeda went to his house to pick him up. She innocently asked a family member, who was there, about her father. Her uncle thought she had discovered the truth. She hadn't. The secret came out. She confronted everyone who was involved in the secret. The color of her skin now made sense. She was many shades darker than the rest of the family.

Later, back at home, her mother still attempted to deny the truth. However, she overheard her mother on the phone demanding that the family member keep the secret. Makeda insisted that they tell the truth.

"What if we had had sex," Makeda said she demanded of her parents. "Neither could answer."

"Hate formed in my heart," Makeda stated.

Worse, it was left up to her to tell the relative that she liked why they could no longer date. He also was in the dark as to their relationship. However, all the family knew the truth, according to Makeda.

Makeda went to her grandfather's house for a short time to live with him. However, he was having financial difficulties. She moved back home where a family member again attempted to have sex with her. She filed a formal complaint. He was taken to jail.

Her mother borrowed money for his bail.

Shortly thereafter, while at school, Makeda began shouting that she wanted to die. A girlfriend told her high school counselor, who called the police. The first officer on the scene comforted her. She wanted to know was she just made to suffer at the hands of the penis men. The policeman assured her that she didn't have to die.

Makeda was so emotionally shattered that she wanted the world around her to disappear including herself. She was hospitalized. She was 18.

However, God was in control. It was not her time.

The dark dusky beauty of Makeda's skin tone reminds one of Solomon's song about the woman he loved. This woman is described as having been kissed by the sun.

Only once before have I seen such a magnificent skin color.

A friend and I were on vacation in Aruba. On walking into the hotel lobby, everyone came to a tongue-tied stop. The gentlemen in front of us could barely give his reservation and name for staring. Me too.

The skin tone of the concierge desk clerk was a velvet smooth jet black that highlighted her high cheekbones. Slim but perfectly shaped in figure, her long hair was pulled back in a professional bun. She was approximately a strategic 5 foot 10 or 11. Her teeth glistened like white polished pearls. It was not difficult to imagine that this is what the Queen of Sheba must have looked like to Solomon. History records state that *Makeda* is one of Queen Sheba's many names.

Makeda is stunningly tall and beautiful after her namesake. But it was not her looks that drew my attention when we met. It was her voice. God has truly gifted her with an ability that brings an audience to its feet.

During our interview, she said her faith was great as a child to the point that when she asked the mountain to move, she expected it to move. However, by the age of 16 she had rejected the concept and doctrine of local churches. She explained why.

"Everybody was in church when I was a child," she said. "Everybody lied and all were okay with the falsehoods."

After being released from the hospital, her godmother sent her to the East Coast to be with her god sisters. She was answering the phone at a fundraiser when she met a lady who prophesied to her about her singing career. A friend had told her that Makeda could really sing. Later, she was approached by two men, twin brothers. They gave her a job with their production company.

They played worldly music but they were biblical scholars. Before and after jazz sessions, they ministered to Makeda about her value to God. They called him *Yah.*

"For the first time in my life, I *heard* the Lord," she said. "I knew or sensed, the familiarity of the name *Yah.* It made me accept their teaching."

She saw them as her family. During breaks they would study and talk about Yahweh. More so, before playing at worldly events, they would pray.

"They would read the Bible with such authority and knowledge that it was impressed upon me that they knew God for themselves on a personal level," she stated.

Makeda acknowledges that they instructed her to study the Bible and stop just rereading it. They studied in parks, at their homes, at the lake, and many other locations.

"On Saturdays, our meal was often fish and grits while we studied," Makeda said with a tender smile of remembrance.

At times, Makeda would return to local churches to try and find out who she is in Christ.

"All the time before, on Sundays, when the pastor hooped and hollered, I never came into any true knowledge of God's truth," she stated with an emphatic nod of her head. "But, traveling around with these brothers, my faith grew until I had a totally different perspective of God. The Bible became a living part of my life."

According to the scriptures, a parent's encouragement causes children to dream of their futures. In today's society, one child wants to be a fireman, another a nurse, another the CEO of a company, and so on.

On the other hand, child abuse is more than exterior physical bruises. When the abuser is a parent or relative, that child's identity and the ability to meld into society is altered. And, more often than not, the God-given abilities to love or dream often cease to function. Instead, they simply learn to survive. However, when the abuser is a professing Christian, the maltreatment cracks the soul of a child like an eggshell. The result is the rejection of church, church doctrine, and people.

It is written that when true believers gather together, it is for the purpose of inspiring and encouraging each other in their walk of Faith,

Hebrews 10: 24-25.

But there is another consequence. Spiritual isolation which God never intended.

Makeda and I are almost three decades apart in age. Yet, we both arrived at the same conclusion that it was the people at fault due to the abuse we endured at the hands of professing Christians. Thus, the solution in both cases was to avoid both people and church.

This is what the devil wants. Nevertheless, he failed.

How is it possible to hear the same story over and over? It is no longer a secret. Yahovah, our heavenly God and Father, had Moses write the stories for us that we could know His truth.

Women, *mothers*, professing to believe in God, traumatize their children because they never knew their own value or destiny.

We have an enemy. Jesus repeated this warning. This enemy's intent is to kill, steal, and destroy, mankind.

God called me into the body of Christ, out of the darkness of Satan's kingdom, when my T-shirt advertised that I was an over the hill senior. Regardless, it was the perfect time, in God's plan, for us to meet. However, Makeda's story was different. She had known God, and or had heard of God since childhood. Yet, we both ended up in the same place due to a mother's lack of knowledge of her importance to God.

Throughout the years, it has become clear to me that God has a sense of humor. He will often show us his truth in unexpected ways. Makeda's life was about to change again.

In approximately 1997, Makeda moved to California onto Crenshaw Boulevard. She saw the move in a dream. However, before she could get a singing contract, she ran out of money. She and the children that she had at that time moved into a shelter.

"My faith never wavered," she emphasized. "I knew I was not going back."

Events came to pass that showed her that was not the location for her. A man came to the shelter one day with a gun looking for his wife. Makeda said she lay on top of her babies to protect them. Later, after looking at a map, Moreno Valley, Ca. caught her attention. They moved. She was able to get an apartment for two months with the help of a voucher.

The city was still undeveloped. However, the area included a day care facility. Out of money, she would walk and look for cash lying on the street. One day she ended up with two dollars that enabled her to buy two packages of noodles, two juices and crackers for her children.

"I heard God say that this is the last time I will have to do this," she said. "He said I would never experience this again."

On yet another occasion, her life was threatened by violence while she was still living on the East Coast. A man was getting ready to shoot her. Suddenly, he gave her a strange look and asked whether she was the lady who sang at a local club. She said yes. He didn't pull the trigger.

She met two young ladies on her new job in Moreno Valley. They told her about an apartment complex in which one of the young girls lived. She got the apartment. On the east coast the twin brothers of the production company had been her family. In California, she was by herself except for her children. She welcomed the young ladies as her new family.

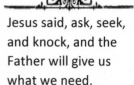

During her search for the truth as to her identity and purpose in this world, she states that she was told do not ask God.

Jesus said, ask, seek, and knock, and the Father will give us what we need,

Matthew 7: 7-11.

I understand. When people do not truly understand God's love, this is often their response. I was told the same thing many times until I learned the truth.

"I had great faith as a child," Makeda stated with a laugh. "Thus, I could not understand the attacks and tribulation. I was a kingdom child. Yet, no one seemed able to explain why I was being persecuted."

Some years before, a lady walked up to Makeda in a bar and said *God loves you*. She thought the woman was crazy. After all, she was sitting in a bar with a cigarette hanging out of her mouth, and a drink in her hand.

The passage of time has taught her that the woman did not lie.

Makeda has six children. All but one was born outside of marriage.

"The father of my sons was a wonderful man and father, but we never married," she said in a fit of laughter. "I could not bring myself to give authority over my life to a *penis* man."

God in control knew different.

Makeda is now married. She feels she finally got it right with a *penis man*. She still calls men by this name.

She has accomplished in her family what she had never received — the gift of unconditional love. During this interview, I watched all of her children walk into the room and greet and hug their mother. Their love for her was obvious.

The gift of faith, along with the ability to love, was instilled in Makeda at birth. It made her a target of the devil. Thus, Satan sent Makeda on a journey that would have broken many others.

The enemy failed because he cannot nullify the plan of God. Plainly, when God is for you, who can be against you. That includes the devil.

Makeda calls her journey a *boot camp* for life. She wrote a song titled *No Greater Love*. It is based on her experience that God stayed with her.

Her youngest child is her daughter. She is eight years old. The light of innocence on her daughter's face as she intertwined her arms around her mom brought a smile to my face. Makeda stopped talking to me and responded in kind to the love of her child. When asked does she think about her life when she looks at her daughter, she said yes.

"I think about it all the time," Makeda stated. "At that same age, I was a veteran sex toy for men. I do everything in my power to keep my daughter safe."

Makeda and I met at a church where she was part of a celebration for the pastor. He was a personal friend. They had met at a conference. Thereafter, he encouraged her to expand her singing career.

The day we met, she was dressed in an African style headdress and outfit with matching earrings. Prior to performing, her short synopsis of her background led me to ask if I could write her story. This is it.

"I feel God is giving me a spiritual whipping because I was supposed to tell my story," she said.

She wrote her first gospel song in 2001. The name of her album is *Naked Truth*. Through the gift of song, Makeda travels the world.

"Once upon a time, my life and my background kept getting me thrown out of the local churches," Makeda said as she burst out in laughter. "Now, my knowledge of who I am allows me to walk into religious buildings around the world without fear because I no longer worship a building, the franchise, or the governmental doctrines of man-made churches."

Every woman's story of abuse and survival is unique and different. Yet the story is the same. No, this is not a contradiction.

The most important person in a child's life, especially daughters, is the mother. And yet, in each case, whether good or bad, as seen in *We Are One*, it is the mother who either builds up her child in the knowledge of God. Or, she sent her spiraling down into a hellish life.

However, in *spiritual truth*, it is not the woman. It is about the devil's influence in the life of spiritually lost women.

Unknowingly, these mothers, who lacked the knowledge of their importance to God, are the instruments that Satan uses to destroy the coming generation, as in this next story.

Chapter 11 Study Guide

From personal experience, I understand Makeda's story. My mother was also a professing Christian. My mother sat on a church pew for 60 years. My mother's father was a traveling preacher.

Nevertheless, my mother never knew that she was valuable in God's eyes.

Nor did she ever understand her true purpose.

1. The question is, how do women continually attend local churches to *hear the gospel of Jesus Christ*, and yet never understand their rightful, Godly, place in His kingdom?

   a. What do you think is the cause?

2. Freedom is promised for everyone, Matthew 11: 28-30.

   a. Why aren't women free?

      i. Are women being kept hostage?

      ii. If yes, how? Discuss.

Notes:

Chapter 12 – A Second Chance Trooper

The Word of God was written for a believer's benefit,
that we through patience and comfort of the scriptures
might have hope, Romans 15: 4

Television shows, in particular, used to depict family life as perfect. It consisted of a father, a mother, and two children, and so forth. The birth of babies usually showed a loving father either fainting in the delivery room, or pacing the outside corridor as his wife gives birth. Then, the father stands grinning by the side of the wife. Both are infatuated with the baby in the mother's arms. They are fascinated by the miniature human being that has all five fingers on each hand and five toes on each foot.

However, reality has a habit of shattering that picture-perfect depiction of a family.

Liza G., born in San Bernardino, California of Mexican, American, Italian parents, had no way of knowing what lay ahead.

One of her older sisters had been so brutally beaten by her father that she ended up in a mental institution for a time. Her father died when Liza was three years old. In order for the family to survive, her mother began to deal with a number of men who gave her money to help pay the bills. There were consequences.

Liza was sexually abused on more than one occasion. She became promiscuous. Nevertheless, by the age of nine or ten,

Liza could recite every Catholic prayer by memory. But she also knew there was no God.

Abuse is a thief. Innocence is its target.

Liza's mother was seldom home. Growing up without parental guidance, she raised herself. Her mother would stop by the house and bring groceries and leave, according to Liza. There was no control and no one to teach her about self-value. More importantly, no one taught her about her value to God.

Liza grew up with the concept of self-gratification, which is directly out of Satan's playbook. There was no one to whom she owed accountability.

Later in life, a friend suggested that she go to church. Liza stated that she always knew about God. But she admits she did not really know God. She began to attend a Christian church in Oceanside, California where she learned about the consequences of abuse.

"Abuse does more than leave scars on your body," she said. "Your soul, your emotions, the way you think, are all influenced. It doesn't matter what you tell yourself, the lack of self-value controls."

Eventually, she began to attend a church in Alta Loma. The message made her cry. She continued for a while but eventually she went back to her old behavior.

Liza had gotten married during her young adulthood. They had a child. Her husband was in the military and deployed several times during their marriage. However, he was not a faithful husband. Nonetheless, his infidelity was never discussed. When they were intimate as husband and wife, Liza simply considered it just having sex. Intimacy on the basis of love was an unknown concept. Eventually they divorced. She remarried and had another child. However, it also ended in divorce.

Her children are aware of her background. Strangely enough it still had an effect on both. Each thought they were born as a result of an unmarried relationship. Liza had to reassure both that she was married when they were conceived.

Children form their own understanding of the life around them. Facts often do not play a part in their perception.

Despite the reality of her background, Liza lathers affection on both of her children. Their pictures are posted all around her desk. And, she has no problem with pointing them out.

Liza should have graduated from high school in 1981. But without any adult guidance, she didn't bother going to school. In 2015, Liza returned to get her GED. Over the past several years, she has been working at a job that usually requires a bachelor degree.

"I truly believe that God opened this door of employment," Liza stated. "Nothing else explains my ability to get this job?"

Liza is more than a survivor. She is also a hustler to get ahead. She acknowledges that she was once addicted to drugs. At a certain point, she made a decision that addiction would not be her life. She grabbed that demonic habit by the horns—if you will—and wrestled it to the ground. She won. The changes in her life clearly demonstrate that she accomplishes her goals.

Years of personal experience with God allow me to add a little more to this story. It is my belief that God would not have put Liza in this position unless He knew she was qualified. He knew she was smart. She had to step up and grow into that particular *shoe* of knowledge about herself. It is a quality that comes through when you speak with her.

Liza and I met through her job. Her expertise in her field of employment is impressive. However, that is not what caught my attention about Liza. It was an extraordinary event where God took control to handle a personal situation in my life.

It is written in the word of God that King David prayed to Yahweh our heavenly father to order his steps in His word. On this particular day, that was my prayer prior to walking into Liza's office. Guidance as to the direction to take was needed from above.

During our discussion, Liza reached over to one corner of her desk and picked up a daily devotion book. She asked if she could read the one for that day aloud. I agreed.

My answer from God was in that devotion.

Today, she and her daughter attend church services regularly. One day Liza thought they would be late to church. Her daughter took the initiative and made sure they were not tardy for service.

Like many teenagers, Liza's daughter thought she would like the new birth control that they put under the skin. She had it done. However, she came back to her mother to let her know she had it removed. In contrast to her own upbringing, Liza and her daughter are able to communicate about anything and everything, including sexual activity, for which Liza is grateful.

Liza's mother is still alive.

"We have a sort of relationship," Liza acknowledged. "However, my mother is very negative so I limit our time together. Conversations with her are as though she is still living in the past. I cannot do that. My life is now in the future with Jesus."

When asked how does she see herself today, Liza replied as follows.

"I am amazed that God loves me like he does," she stated. "Especially given what he knows about me."

During our time together, Liza repeated a quote, which I love.

"What people think about me is none of my business."

We sat there laughing hilariously at the thought of using this saying in response to nosy people. She doesn't remember where she heard it but she likes it because it says so much in a few words.

It is my opinion, given today's social media madness of people meddling in another person's business, that this quote should be everybody's quote. On the other hand, the stark eye-opening reality of this adage is that *if* those who have committed suicide over opinions, had practiced living in the truth of this quote, perhaps they would still be alive. It is almost beyond belief that interfering people, who cannot control their own world, yet take deliberate steps to drive another human being to take their own life because someone does not like them.

During the recording of Liza's story of victory, two goals were discussed. First, she believes that she is destined to be a speaker, particularly to women who have been abused. Second, she would like to be a missionary. She believes that the gifts that God wants her to share are kindness, care, and compassion.

Her desire to be a missionary brought up an important point. Initially, Liza acknowledged that she did not believe that knowledge of the Scriptures was necessary to have faith in God. However, the reminder of how God used her book of devotion of scriptures to help me gave her inspiration to see things from God's point of view.

God used her to *read His Word* to help me. In other words, business intellect had not helped. However, the minute she read the devotion, I *knew* God had given His answer.

God's message changed everything. His scriptural advice was heeded.

We read a few more scriptures, such as *Matthew 4:4* that also point out the need to know His Word. Jesus often prayed to the Father. But, in this one recorded prayer, He says something very unique in *John 17*. It is an eternal petition for all believers. It explains how a believer's Faith grows through knowing the Word.

Liza is not wasting time to implement her goals. At the time of this interview, she had already signed up for a ministry class that her church sponsors. It will run two years. At the end, she will receive a certificate of ministry.

Instructing our children in the declarations and promises of God is similar to surrounding them with a safety net of protection whether they are asleep or awake.

Proverbs 6: 20-22

"I am so excited about this ministry class," Liza said. "I believe second chances are a favorite past time of God because I was given a second chance at [true] life. But, first things first. I have to pass an assessment test."

Liza is right. My own testimony, as well as the other stories in this book, are proof that Yahweh is a second-chance God through Faith in His Son Jesus.

Over the years, it has been said many times by certain famous people, who have a platform before the world, that there was no guide book in how to raise children when they were growing up. In direct contrast, God left specific directions about how to treat your family in His recorded Word—the Bible. More specifically, His instructions are clear about the importance of a mother's instructions in the lives of

Jesus prays for us, all future believers in Him, as our faith grows through the study of the written words of the disciples, that we may ALL be One, as He and the Father are One, [in mind, righteousness and love]
John 17: 20-22.

her children. Additionally, they literally watch over our children during the night and guide them when they are awake.

Our heavenly Father left no stone unturned to warn us about the danger of misused words. Throughout the Bible, words caused wars, murder, incest, and especially disobedience to God.

For 60 years my mother remained a member of a local church that preached the protocol of unworthiness of God's love and mercy. For 60 years, up to her death, she repeated those words about herself. The consequence was horrific, as shown in both of my previous books. The *spirit* of Satan ruled and reigned in her life until her death.

In plain English, Satan *spiritually* killed my mother in her twenties although we didn't bury her until she was 86. She never understood that the *media concept* of weapons of mass destruction are not always made of cold, hard steel.

The status of the world today proves that the *true* weapons of mass destruction are Words.

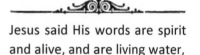

Jesus said His words are spirit and alive, and are living water,

John 4:10; 6: 63.

When God first spiritually awakened me to His presence, His Word seemed to jump off of the page, as though they were alive. Now, it makes sense. God was spoon feeding me with His Word. As we grow, knowledge of the Word grows with us. They become like rungs on a step ladder. More so, faith in the Word of God makes the past the bottom rung.

However, false religiosity has taken God's Word and twisted it to make it fit their particular doctrine. This in turn leaves the people of God caught between *the Rock* and a hard place and unable to trust God or His Word.

The bottom line is, *it ain't over till God says it's over.*

The story coming up co-signs this truth.

Chapter 12 Study Guide

The Bible is full of stories of redemption for people from all walks of life, including adultery, conspiracy to commit murder, to betrayal, to selling your own brother to slave runners, and much more. But, why does it seem a given that the parents pass this same spirit down into their children?

    1. Do you know anyone who acts exactly like their parent in a negative manner?

        a. How do you think this happened?

        b. What did you do?

    2. Women and men kill their children and spouses.

        a. Why?

        b. The answer is in God's Word.

            i. Find and Discuss.

Notes:

Chapter 13 –A Divine Loosing
of Binding Tentacles

God still breaks the chains of bondage, no matter
how long they have been in place, Luke 13: 12.

The endless search by children looking for long-lost parents proves that a judicial ruling cannot cut the parental umbilical cord. Sonja Rideout's story shows that not even death can sever the invisible soul-ties between a mother and her child. It doesn't matter whether the relationship was good, bad, or ugly.

Like the tentacles of an octopus at the bottom of the ocean, the almost lethal chokehold of unhealthy possessiveness reached up from the grave to twist around Sonja's heart. God sent a friend to rescue her.

We met in a business setting. During a meeting with one of her associates, Sonja Rideout, 51, African-American, came in and joined the discussion.

The first impression of Sonja was outstanding. Not a hair was out of place. Her beautiful, well-manicured hands, her perfect makeup, and clothing, were striking. However, the Holy Spirit led me to *hear* what was yet to be spoken.

Her exterior perfection was a mask to hide the pain of her existence. During our interview, she acknowledged that she had been spiritually and emotionally choking to death. And, the battle was still raging.

I understood. Once upon a time, before God intervened in my life, I was like Sonja. My books, *Mine, an everlasting promise of love, deliverance, and wholeness,* and *Purposely Unchained,* demonstrate the process that is divinely required to move out of demonic bondage and into the light and love of Jesus.

The thought occurred as I wrote this chapter that perhaps the glossy exteriors, the enormous church hats, the brilliant dresses and suits, etc. are a mask. We women tend to look so good on the outside that no one will think to dig deeper. If not for the Holy Spirit of God, it would not have occurred to me to really *hear* Sonja's pain behind the beautiful exterior.

Both of her parents were teachers. However, they separated when Sonja was two years old. The family began to suffer financially. They seldom had sufficient food. At one point, Sonja's grandmother became ill. Her mother flew to Phoenix to take care of her. Her aunt took over Sonja's care.

Things became easier on a financial level when Sonja was six years old. Her mother began to date one man in particular. By the age of 13 or 14, her mother began to insist that Sonja call him daddy. Sonja refused. It did not make sense to her. She knew they were not married. It caused problems in their relationship.

During this time, her mother never talked about God, faith, nor Jesus to Sonja. Her grandmother did prior to her death. Nor did her mother talk about her personal life when she was a young woman or a child except for one time. They were watching the movie *Mississippi burning.*

The movie reminded her mother of the time that she and the other children had to walk around a white neighborhood to get to their school. It turned a 15-20-minute walk into an hour's journey.

From personal experience in talking with people who were raised especially in the South, this was not unusual. Most refused to talk about it. Sonja's mother was just one of probably millions who choose to forget the foolishness of prejudice and the effect on their lives. Nevertheless, time reveals they paid an emotional toll which then transferred to the following generations.

Sonja was eleven when they moved to Los Angeles. The family attended church two times a year—once at Christmas, and again at Easter with an aunt and uncle. She attended summer Bible school where she had to learn to recite *Luke 9:23* in front of the entire congregation at the end of summer school.

"I can recite it even to this day," Sonja said. "But I never had a true understanding of what it meant."

We discussed the meaning of this verse. In simple terms, Jesus was saying that we cannot live life any way we choose and then claim to be His follower. The various trials and tribulations of the first disciples, i.e. learners, clearly demonstrate the seriousness of this Scripture.

Jesus said to all [believers], if anyone desires to follow me, they must deny themselves, and take up the cross [of obedience] and follow him, **Luke 9: 23.**

Her mother's male companion was at their house two to three days a week. He attended her graduation from both elementary and high school. Sonja was 14 when her mother revealed the truth as to why he was not there all the time. He was married.

Whenever her mother would try to form a relationship with other men, her car would suddenly have broken windows and flattened tires. Her mother always returned to the married man. Her reason was that he took care of them. To Sonja, they had stuff, because of this man. However, he always used profanity around Sonja. Nevertheless, her mother insisted that he deserved respect. This continued up until Sonja was 18 when she insisted to her mother that she had a right to her own opinion.

At one point, when Sonja was around 30, her mother made it clear that she would not leave this man. However, she told Sonja that she could leave. More so, her mother rejected a better job in order to stay in a relationship with this man. Sonja stayed.

Sonja wanted to get married. She fell in love with a gentleman in the military. However, it didn't work out. She thought perhaps the failure of the relationship was due to her weight. She joined a weight loss program and lost weight. Eventually, she gained it all back. She made a decision.

"Anyone who wants me will take me as I am, weight and all," she said. "If they truly love me, my weight won't matter."

Many of us have been there. The problem with this concept is that despite the declarations, many women do not accept themselves. Time would reveal this truth in Sonja's life.

Her mother suggested the she find a man like the one she had, the philanderer, because he was a good man. Eventually, Sonja found a man.

He was worse.

God did not leave us in the dark without an answer. More so, in relation to this scripture, it also states that *they who love it* [the words of death or life] *will eat of it.*

It is written that words either speak life into the ears of the hearer, or death.

Women often wonder how they end up being exactly like their mothers, whether it is good, bad, or just plain ugly. It is due to the words

Proverbs 18: 21.

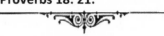

that are spoken into our ears, our souls, our hearts.

Plainly speaking, we *eat* the words of mothers because we *love* them, as in the case of Sonja. Thus, the spoken words *of people we love* mold us as though we are pliable clay on a sculptor's table. This explains the past, the present and the future, whether good, bad, or ugly. We either ate death, or we were fed life.

From personal experience, this was also very true in my life. Regardless of how hard I tried, it seemed that I imitated my mother's character throughout my life. It was baffling until God revealed His truth that is recorded in His Word.

The lack of *godly* training in how to love and value herself, led to a loveless life for my mother. I had *spiritually eaten* her words. Thus, I did the same until God intervened.

Sonja knew that she wanted something different than her mother's life. She wanted a man who would love her for herself. She accepted a proposal but then something told her to question the relationship. It ended. However, her desire for a husband remained.

"Did you really know anything about love," I asked.

Her response was enlightening.

"The only thing I knew about love was my mother's faithfulness to a married man because of the stuff he bought her," she said. "It didn't matter if that man belonged to another woman."

We discussed the word of God where it is stated that we are to first love God and then ourselves second. In other words, Jesus taught that we are more valuable than the birds, the flowers of the field, and even animals. Accepting—if you will—another woman's leftovers is not understanding or loving ourselves. More so, this type of advice from a mother brings into question their relationship.

"I think my mother and I had a loving relationship," she said.

"How," I asked.

We discussed the word of God as to His instructions about teaching children, especially the daughters. Sonja was surprised to find that God had left such specific directions.

On April 25, 2010, her mother was admitted into the hospital where she was put on a respirator. Sonja was in her mid-forties. Her mother had never told Sonja that she was sick. Sonja felt that she was left out of the loop. After returning home, Sonja received a call that her mother would not survive.

"I hung up the house phone, picked up my cell phone and car keys and walked into the closed garage," she said. "After turning on both cars, I sat in one and waited."

A coworker called Sonja on her cell phone. She asked her what she was doing. Sonja replied that she was driving. She remembers feeling as though she was in a trance, as though she were not really there. She remembers thinking *God will take care of my mother and I am no longer needed.*

However, God had other plans for her life. He sent a *helper.*

"I heard this loud knocking on the garage door as her friend called out to the paramedics," Sonja stated. "I did not want to go to the hospital but they insisted."

During the ride, the ambulance attendant told her that her life was valuable and she should not have tried to commit suicide. She explained that she was scared. Her mother had not wanted to go to the hospital. Sonja insisted. Her mother got worse and died. Sonja felt responsible.

She was released after a few days. Both the doctor and a relative tried to reassure her that her mom's death was not her fault.

More to the point, Sonja had never been alone. Sonja admits that she didn't do well at living the single life.

"Basically, I went wild," she stated with a grin. "At the age of 42 I realized I could stay out late, run around town, invite people in, all without having to give an account of my behavior."

Just as God had plans for her, so did the devil.

About a year after the death of her mother, she met a man at a roller-skating rink. Lacking true *godly* mother wit, they exchanged information. On the surface, he looked good. His mannerisms were that of a gentleman. He drove a nice car. However, time would reveal that his *spirit* was truly demonic.

Everything that he claimed to be true was a lie, including his real name. He had also stated that he owned his own business. Over time, Sonja loaned him a considerable amount of money on more than one occasion. Each time he promised repayment. It never happened. Eventually, he asked for a set of keys to her home. Meanwhile, he suggested that they get married. She said no. Her denial resulted in a yelling match. Unaware yet of the darkness of his soul, she ended their relationship. Shortly thereafter she would discover the truth.

A friend called and told Sonja and asked her to go to a particular website. Her former boyfriend was listed as a registered sex offender. The police were looking for him. Thereafter, she was required to take a test for HIV. His full history included the fact that he had been in prison for raping women at knife point. Lastly, he was already married. He was later arrested.

In many cases like this, the woman feels at fault. Sonja was no different.

"I felt dumb because I valued him more than myself."

We discussed a single truth that was like an elephant in the room. How *could* she know her godly value when her example chose another woman's husband—for years—as her companion.

God designed a process for those of us who were not taught our value when we were children. This specialized training course is in my book: *Purposely Unchained.*

We discussed how my story is a testimony to this truth. For instance, God took a former nonbeliever, an atheist, and instructed, changed, and *corrected*, his daughter—me—until I understood. What was He doing? He was remolding me into the image of His son Jesus. More so, He made it clear that feelings of guilt are from Satan.

At first, Sonja could not visualize life without her mother. Today, she realizes that God has plans for her.

Currently, she is not yet attending services at local churches. Instead, she listens to online sermons.

"I need to learn about myself and my value to God," she stated. "I need to just be still and heal and understand that God does truly love me."

Her reluctance is understandable. We discussed the importance of being around godly people as a support system.

Over the years, it has been said many times by certain people, who have a platform before the world, that there was no guide book in how to raise children when they were growing up. Several years ago, an admission by a grown child clarified the true consequences of this ideology.

An adult child always commented that they were just like their parent *in the past* rather than the *new* life of their parent as a Christian. Their explanation was yet a surprise. The *memory* of how their parent used to act was stronger because they had *years* to watch and absorb our behavior. *Ouch.*

In contrast to the ungodly perception that God failed to leave instructions for His creation, God left specific directions about how to raise a family. More specifically, His instructions are clear about the importance of a mother's directions in the lives of her children. Better yet, God promises in His Word that His instructions will literally watch over our children during the night and guide them when they are awake.

When God first spiritually awakened me to His presence, His Word would sometimes seem to jump off of the page, as though they were alive. Now, it makes sense. God was spoon feeding me with His Word. Knowledge of the Word grows in our hearts.

The Word is like seeds planted in a garden. Our minds are the ground. When mature, faith and truth are so strong, they cannot be uprooted by life.

However, religiosity has taken God's Word and decided to *re*interpret it to make it fit their particular doctrine. This in turn leaves the people of God caught between *the Rock* and a hard place. Worse, they are unable to trust God or His Word.

From personal experience, I know that His Word has never changed, for which I am forever grateful. If not for the eternal veracity of His Word, my life would not have been transformed twenty-four years ago.

God said His Word is like fire, and like a hammer that breaks up rocks. The roots of ungodly thinking, from the many years spent as an atheist, required both. In other words, the utilization of God's word ripped apart my ungodly thoughts, fired them up, and put a hammer to them — when necessary — in order to bring me into my Godly purpose.

God called the Body of Christ out of darkness for a reason. The world, the lost, are waiting.

Romans 8: 15-19.

Through the guidance of the Holy Spirit, the Word of God made sense of my life. Thus, the attempt to *re*interpret His Word is not of God.

The story of love reaching out from the grave to those left behind is a favorite story-line from movies. In the case of Sonja, it came true. Nonetheless, God intervened.

Sonja survived. She is now learning to walk and live in the unchanged promise that God always viewed her as valuable, hence Jesus dying on the Cross — for her. This is a truth that should be repeated daily by the body of Christ.

Jesus made a comment during His ministry on earth. He told His disciples that the harvest, the spiritually lost people, was truly huge. But the workers were sparse. Today, mothers are killing their children, or allowing boyfriends to slay their own offspring. And worse, children are killing children.

Where are the laborers?

Death is not always physical, as in Sonja's case.

Nevertheless, the harvest, the lost, is abounding in size. Something, or someone, is missing, and has been for a long time.

My question is *Where are the Sons of God*?

Today, in many cities, there seems to be a local church on every block, on every corner, in vacant storefronts, and now even in hotel rooms.

Yet, the question remains. Where are the Sons of God?

Chapter 13 Study Guide

1. Motherly love that emotionally cripples a child is more common than one would think. Why? Because on the exterior, it often takes on the form of simply loving the child by spoiling them.

    a. Do you know of someone like the mother in this chapter that seemed to love her children but in actuality was emotionally choking them to death?

    b. Do you think the mother is buying love from her child?

    c. Do you think a mother's emotional hold on her children has something to do with how she views her own value?

2. In most cases, the behavior of the grown children reveals the spiritual truth behind this type of erroneous love.

    a. Do you know of a now grown child who is unable to function in life and still depends on their parent for guidance?

        i. What do you think is the solution? Can this type of mother-bondage be broken?

            1. Discuss

Notes:

Chapter 14 – The Lost are Waiting

When a believer is Led in their lives by the Holy Spirit of God, they are the Children of God. The world is waiting. **Romans 8: 13-14, 16-19**

At first glance across the room, onlookers saw a beautiful, slender, woman. She stood up to pose a question to a panel member at the conference. Her quiet demeanor matched her impeccable dialogue. However, something about her caught my attention.

We met afterwards. For privacy sake, I will call her *Many* because her story represents *many* women. The interview revealed a startling tale. Some of the invisible wounds had not healed.

During her childhood, three words linked together had formed a single sentence that was used like a battering-ram. It cracked and broke her spirit like a twig on the ground that we step upon. And, as in the lives of *many* women, the wielder of the weapon was not a stranger.

Many's mother replaced the word *no* with *You are nothing.* For some unknown reason, she had determined that her daughter's life had no value. The force of those words took root in her heart and soul and grew. They ate away at *Many's* self-esteem more efficiently than acid into metal.

"I learned to laugh early on in order to keep others from seeing how worthless I really felt," she said during our meeting. "I have never told anyone before you."

Her polished smiling veneer covered a stunning darkness.

By the time she turned 13, instead of dreaming about boyfriends and teenage get togethers, she was spending her time in a mental hospital. She had been committed by her mother because she told that she had been molested by her grandfather. After her release, she was homeless.

She acknowledged that she did anything and everything in order to survive on the streets. The use of drugs and over-eating soothed the pain of her existence. Slightly built, probably a size 6, it was difficult to believe that at one time *Many* had weighed over 300 pounds several years back.

"I keep a picture of what I looked like then pasted on my refrigerator, as a reminder," she said. "A person can only eat so much. Drugs took up where the food left off."

She had the first of her four children at 19.

"I took whatever job I needed to do," she stated with an emphatic nod of her head. "I did it to take care of them, from topless dancing to bookkeeping. I didn't care."

During the recounting of her past, it became evident that in spite of her belief about herself, *Many* made sure that her children knew they were loved.

"Despite my absolute belief about my own unworthiness, I made it a point to teach my children everything opposite of what my mother had said to me," she said.

Her determination paid off. At the time of this interview, all of her children were academic honor students. *Many*, Caucasian, then 42, said she sobered up at 32, and had been clean and sober since. However, her life took a dramatic turn at the age of 38.

Many was working as a bookkeeper. But, despite her skill, she could not progress because of the lack of a formal degree. *Many* said she realized she needed more education when she was rejected for a raise despite her ability.

"Convinced that I was dumb, I tried a different tactic," she commented. "One of my co-workers was a college student. I secretly read and studied her books for a year and a half, until she caught me. However, it was not helping me on my job."

The memory made her laugh.

The co-worker, whose books *Many* had been studying, dared her to enroll in college. In a true-grit show of determination, one that would rival John Wayne for that title, *Many* took the dare. She enrolled in college.

"I was terrified," *Many* admitted with a mischievous grin. "I had heard it so often that it had sunk in that I was too stupid to learn."

To the contrary, *Many* would graduate with *two* Associates Degrees in a few months from the time of this interview. In addition, she was already accepted by a college to complete her Bachelor's Degree. One of her children was also graduating at the same time with her Associates.

Three new words had become *Many's* fight song.

"Yes I can!" she shouts from the rooftops.

However, *Many* acknowledged that it was difficult to believe that God loved her due to her life. On the other hand, it seemed that education had saved her life.

This concept is unnervingly common in the educational world. And, it is also well-known that some professors deliberately challenge the beliefs of Christians.

College campus life seems to loudly announce two facts. Parental guidance has failed. And, the *Sons of God* are still missing. Not to worry. Gangland mentality has filled the gap.

Given the uncountable acts of molestation at home, at school, at work, and at play, the young women of today are fighting back. However, the cost is great. In a number of instances, the price is a woman's femininity.

Today, it is *cool* to smell of armpit musk rather than Pure Crystal perfume, my favorite. Several years ago, victorious and fresh from battle, three young women reveled in the blinding spotlight of alleged fame and conquest on a social media outlet. However, an almost collective audible gasp of dismay ricocheted around the world as people watched the sheer rage of a bar room brawl take place in *Petticoat Junction,* if you will.

No longer sweet, like sugar and spice, three 14-year-old young women pre-planned a vicious attack. It was deliberately taped for exhibition to the world. After what seemed like several right-left hooks to the jaw of the 13-year-old victim, followed by actual Karate kicks to her head, that would have made Bruce Lee proud, these young women claimed triumph.

Given the vindictiveness of those involved in this particular video, society, often ho-hum in its attitude about brawls, were suddenly concerned that young women are adopting the fighting mentality of male gangs.

The question begs to be asked, "Why the surprise?"

A familiar website explains that a "gang originally was a group of individuals who shared a common identity," such as a group of workmen. Thus, gang originally meant a harmless association of people. Any organization that consisted of a group of people with common needs or purpose was a "gang."

Time has consistently shown that "group/gang" members understood that a group has power, and groups have utilized that power of unity in every walk of life. For instance, under the original meaning of gang, a "posse" who helped the sheriff catch the bad guys was a gang. Cavemen formed a gang for the purpose of hunting and survival. People who were deprived of their rights formed a *gang* to present a united front.

Over time, the positive use of *grouping together* became negative. Today the word gang generally implies groups connected for the purpose of criminal activities.

On the other hand, current day television gives the world a close-up view of the profitability of being involved in a group, i.e. "gang." Without naming names, if you can lie, cheat, and trick/manipulate others—in a group setting—the best liar or cheater receives a monetary award that surpasses a lifetime of weekly payroll checks.

In other words, if you were good at utilizing the tools and spirit of the devil, through your flesh, you won, *Galatians 5: 19-21.*

Someone said a few years back that over 12,000 videos were registered on a social media outlet of girls fighting. The reason doesn't matter. The key word is *fight*. On many of the videos, the male counterparts are on the sidelines cheering on the *so-called* warriors.

The combined desire for equality, in light of the unsuccessful battles by their female predecessors, has made the young women of today shed their femininity like a set of old worn out clothes. However, this current day trend of dressing and acting like a man, in hopes that it will make a difference in how a woman is treated, is an old and ancient error.

Moses was told to command both the men and women to *not* dress in clothing made for the opposite sex because it was morally disgusting to God.

Deuteronomy 22: 5.

It is *not* about the clothes. It is about the *spirit* that is behind this behavior.

The past always contains a lesson, whether we learn from it or not. For instance, what is genocide? And, what does this have to do with the *mental* destruction of the woman's God-ordained purpose?

Food for thought. Everything!

There are two elements of the crime of genocide. One is the *mental* element, meaning the *intent* to destroy, in whole or in part, a particular group. For actions to be considered genocide, they must include *both* the intent and physical acts.

One of the punishable acts of genocide is the causing of mental harm, which includes inflicting trauma on members of the group through widespread intentional actions. The other is physical acts.

Since the beginning of time, man decided he should rule mankind through war, and especially the women. This was not God's original plan, according to His Word. However, the influence of the devil has led the world on this path of hate.

The daughters, plural, worked with their father to rebuild the wall and gates around Jerusalem.

Nehemiah 3: 12

In the world of religion, this same concept is accomplished by reinterpreting and twisting the Word of God until it looks like a pretzel. And if that doesn't work, they simply delete the woman's name, on *numerous* occasions, out of the recorded Word of God.

For instance, *all* the men are specifically named in *Nehemiah 3: 1-32*. Yet, the women remain nameless other than they were female.

We know this is not and was not God's intention. Jesus continually acknowledged women in His ministry. And, the *first* person that He identified Himself to was the Samaritan woman, again no name. More so, I am a 20th century witness to tHis truth that women are an essential part of the Kingdom of Jesus Christ.

A multitude of particulars bring about changes in a person's life, such as the story of *Many*.

She was married at 18 and divorced at 23. She thought she was destined to be a welfare mom.

A lover of poetry, she read "Phenomenal Woman" by Maya Angelou. She began to understand that in order to climb the heights of success, you have to surround yourself with *climbers.*

More importantly, she joined a church group where she met people who helped keep her spiritually grounded. She now surrounds herself with people with positive attitudes. The support of her church members, and the memory of Angelou's words of encouragement, helped her overcome difficult times.

When she first started college, she had no car and had to walk her children to school before making the trek to college. She persevered. When we met, she was currently majoring in sociology and carrying a 3.7 G.P.A.

Encouraging a person to get an education is a good thing. But those who guide people to first know God and thus their own identity in His Kingdom, are the real dream builders.

Jesus gave us the perfect example with the Samaritan woman. He knew everything about her past. Nevertheless, by the time He finished telling her about *living* water, her entire life changed.

In other words, He *first* offered her encouragement and living water. Then, He brought up her background. She was intrigued. Her entire life was changed forever, according to scripture.

My first thought about the water would have probably been *what's in it* to make it alive. Thank God for spiritual knowledge.

The Samaritan woman went back to the men in town and testified about Jesus. Not only did Jesus change her life, but through her, the lives of others were also transformed.

Nevertheless, a few men had to make a snippy response to her fledgling ministry. They informed her that they now believed because they had heard him personally, and *not* because of her testimony. Sound familiar, ladies.

What happened to *thank you?* Or, at the least, not saying anything, *John 4: 39-42.*

The stories in *We Are One* are merely the tip of the iceberg of Satan's unchanged goal to destroy mankind—through women. This is *not* about blaming the woman. This is about the devil's method of achieving his goal. And yes, I was included. The devil used me to harm my children because I lacked knowledge about my *in-built* I.P.S. system.

We—the woman—are the first line of defense. We are the *first* inspiration in a child's life. But and this is a *big* but. If *we* do not know nor understand who *we* are, then it is impossible to teach the essential knowledge of *godly* value to our sons and daughters, *as divinely spoken*. We either send our children out into the world with a *spiritual* umbrella and boat. Or, we send them out to drown without any covering.

Instructing our children in the declarations and promises of God is the same as surrounding them with a safety net of protection whether they are asleep or awake.

Proverbs 6: 20-22

God is omnipotent and all-knowing. He knew these issues would arise. Thus, He left His Word to prepare His soldiers—this includes YOU, the woman.

We Are One takes up Jesus' *spiritual* clarion call to the *Sons of God*.

Stand up. Step up.

The world is waiting. The World *needs* you.

Chapter 14 Study Guide

1. Children are always told to tell if anyone attempts to molest or harm them. Yet, in many instances, children are then blamed for telling.

    a. Do you know of a woman who tried to tell about molestation when she was a child?

    b. Do you know if the parents listened?

    c. If not, what happened to that women in later life?

2. Do you think the manner in which women are discussed in the Bible play a part in why women of today have a trust issue with the Word of God?

    a. Discuss.

3. According to scripture, the devil knows our position of faith.

    a. Do you believe this is true? Discuss.

4. In most cases, the behavior of the children thereafter reveals the consequences of being ignored.

    a. Do you know someone who is unable to function in life today because no one listened when they were a child?

        i. What do you think is the solution?

ii.   Can this break in trust be healed?

1.   Discuss

Notes:

Chapter 15 — Purposed Encourager

Those who are called by God, work
according to His purpose, Romans 8:28

A conference was in process. The audience was mostly comprised of women. It was scheduled that I read the first chapter of my book that was titled, *The Woman, God's Womb of Purpose.* I approached the microphone. However, rather than read from my novel, I presented a question to the audience. They were asked to express their identity, as perceived in their minds. Several responded.

Some gave the titles of their jobs, such as: CEO of such and such company; President of whatever; Director of Human Resources, etc. Others named various religious titles, such as: minister, prophetess, elder, etc.

None said they were purposed by God to *change the world.* In the dream, I began to talk about a woman's divine assignment from God, per His Word.

Upon waking from the dream, the realization was startling. God's truth had been there all the time. A cliché came to mind how the *truth that is hid in plain sight is a greater secret than if it had been buried in the ground.*

The divine commission of writing to encourage God's people was received in 2001. As time passed, my attention focused on women. This dream took place in 2009.

The Word of God makes it clear that Satan went after Eve in the Garden of Eden.

Eve's deception is always preached that this happened because she was the weaker vessel. That was not Satan's reason for making her his target.

The devil went after Eve because he knew she was God's purposed nurturer. And, if *she* could be tricked into getting off of her God destined path, she would change the world.

Scripture shows that is exactly what happened. The world today co-signs this truth. *We Are One* brings it into the light.

Eve mistakenly thought she was helping her husband Adam when she shared Satan's information, i.e. knowledge. The world was changed, but not for the better. Satan also knew that once Eve was off of God's path, she would have children, who would do the same.

Initially, according to scripture, Eve said no. However, what is seldom taught, if ever, is that Satan went into her mind—in a vision—and caused her to *see* evil as pleasant, good, and something that would make her wise. And, as a good *helper* wife would do, she shared this fake good news with her husband.

Plainly, the devil made her literally see, *Hebrew: ra'ah,* in a vision, that the knowledge of evil, *Genesis 3:22,* was good for food, pleasant to the eyes, and would make one wise. It is useless to speculate on why the translators decided to use the word *tree* in place of *knowledge.* Yet, they did not mess with Yahovah's Word in verse 22, where He makes it plain that this is about the *knowledge* of good and evil.

It is not difficult to imagine that many of God's people have experienced both dreams and visions. However, we need to know that everything that God does, the devil tries to imitate. It was so in my case as I revealed in my other books.

For instance, Satan did not wait until I was entrenched, saturated, with the Word of God. He infiltrated my mind twelve hours after my spiritual rebirth. His goal was simple. He challenged God's truthfulness as to His love and faithfulness.

Thus, I understand the devil's questions to Eve whether or not God had told her the truth. Satan's attacks were disconcerting until I learned to discern the difference between his lies and God's truth.

Time, and the study of God's Word, demonstrated that Satan will never give a dream or vision that encourages a child of God to obey God alone. More specifically, from experience, God does not like debt. Thus, any dream or vision that inspires a person to go into debt is not of God, such as my disastrous foray into a building that was unaffordable. Why? Debt is bondage. And, we are to serve only Jesus.

When the woman is unaware of her divine assignment, we negatively extinguish the dreams in our children, as many of the stories in *We Are One* illustrate. In each case, it was the mother who spiritually gave her children to the devil by abandoning them in Satan's system of spiritual disbelief. There, they are taught to believe in only themselves.

The world today, and since the beginning, proves this to be true. Ever since the disobedience of Adam in the Garden of Eden, parents have been killing their wives and children. Today, the trend continues.

It is written that those who have been rescued from the authority of the devil are to tell of the love and mercy of God.

Psalms 107: 2

My life before God consisted of fighting against anyone being in control of my life. Nevertheless, as the seed of a woman who never knew her divine purpose, my choice of a first husband used alcohol to numb his senses due to issues with his mother. In turn, this spiritual discontent passed down to our children.

Nevertheless, God is always in control.

The desire to write about a hero arose in my spirit as a child. I thought that yearning had died due to parental abuse. It didn't. My dream was in hiatus.

Today, I write about the one and only true Hero Jesus. Thus, the call on my life proved that the past *was truly only a pit stop* in my life as God led me into my divine commission. More importantly, the stories in *We Are One* show that our godly assignment is *not* a one-woman thing.

Steadfast Faith in the face of adversity helps the gospel, because it can be seen. And, it encourages other believers.

Philippians 1: 12-14.

Our ordained directive cannot be nullified by the devil, or our past. However, we fall prey to tricks when we do not understand our divine assignment, as a few stories in *We Are One* indicate. We need to be informed.

By the inspiration of the Holy Spirit, I am telling.

My former life as an atheist, for 52 years, would seem to have eliminated me out of the will of God forever. My book: *Mine, An Everlasting Promise of Love, Deliverance, and Wholeness,* demonstrates that I was never out of His authority. More specifically, *Purposely Unchained* demonstrates to the people of God that training is still necessary in this era for all of God's people. The first disciples had to be instructed prior to being sent forth into their mission. Every person called by God must also be educated for their assignment.

God has a unique sense of humor. I still burst into eye-watering fits of laughter when I muse over God's methods of getting his way.

First, He sent His new child, an atheist from the world in every way, to her first church. Although the men were dressed in beautiful finery, the faces of the women were unadorned with makeup and earrings. In addition, they wore long skirts, and blouses with long sleeves. Many of the women truly believed the erroneous messages that they were not worthy.

After awaking from the cocoon of grief of the loss of my husband, I gave in to the insistent requests and did my first testimony.

"Lord I thank you and because of the death and resurrection of Jesus Christ, your son, I must be worthy of your love," I said before sitting down.

God had been working on my mind even while I was encased in a cocoon of grief.

Audible gasps of dismay had fluctuated throughout the church like a shock wave after an earthquake. Afterwards, many of the women would not sit next to me on the pews.

Apostle Paul said that adversity against him actually helped the spread of the good news. God moved me. My message remains unchanged.

Nevertheless, greater is the spoken declaration of our unchanged purpose into our hearts and soul than the devil's tricks.

We Are One TELLS the women of God of the importance of knowing the *truth* of our divine assignment.

Satan must have thought that he had stopped God's plan for our redemption when he influenced people to kill Jesus. He failed. Nor is it difficult to imagine that the devil thinks he has stopped the women of God through acts of abuse, abandonment, etc. But again, the devil fails because greater is He that is *in* us than he that is in the world.

Thousands of years after the new covenant was written, the Holy Spirit reminded me of this verse, and the importance of maintaining and recording our faith journey.

Apostle Paul's assignment was important to the world. Through the writings of a few of the first disciples, and Apostle Paul, we have the recording of the Gospel, the Good News. God made sure that we have the means and way back to Him through Faith in His Son Jesus, *John 17: 19-22.*

Scripture reveals that Satan did everything he could—through people—to kill Paul to stop him from completing his assignment of taking the *Good News* to the non-Jewish nations. That's *you and I.*

The woman's assignment is no less important to the world.

What is it? God declared it, i.e. *He spoke it;* thus, it is so.

First, You—the woman—are God's *helper* to dominate, i.e. *rule* over the animal creatures on earth. But, what about each other? God did *not* leave it to chance.

He gave Adam the authority to name everything. In plain English, it states:

It is written that when we reject God's truth in place of old and familiar doctrine, we are judging ourselves to be unworthy of eternal life.

Acts 13: 44-46.

Genesis 1: 19 - And Yahovah made animals and took them to Adam to see what names he would give them: and whatever he called it, that was its name.

And in Genesis 2: 22, Yahovah took a rib out of Adam and made a female body, which He then took to Adam.

And, verse 23, Adam called her woman.

However, verse 24 reveals a startling truth. Remember, Yahovah said whatever Adam called any living creature, thus it would be so. He first called Eve *'ishshaw* – a female. But when he spoke of a mother, he was speaking of the *purpose* of the female.

In *Genesis 3: 20*, Adam now names his wife *Eve*. In Hebrew it is *Chavvah (or Eve),* i.e. life-giver, because she was the *'em*, the mother, the *bond, the glue* of the family.

The translators used the English word *mother* for 'em.' However, as it often does, the English language loses in translation. The Hebrew word for *mother is 'em,* which means a *female as the bond,* i.e. the pledge, the oath, the glue, *of the family.*

Did you get that Ladies?

In that Adam was created by God from the earth, he is not speaking of his mother. He is the first human creation. Thus, the only *'em* he could be talking about is *Eve.* And from there, every woman throughout history who has the potential to be *the bond, the glue* that holds a family together. Few women have ever understood the divine importance of this announcement.

Satan knew this truth, thus his challenge to Eve in the garden about God speaking the truth. She was the devil's target because of her divine mission to the world.

But there's more. What does this have to do with the adversity and persecution that women face on almost a daily basis? Why the rape, molestation, of women? Why do mothers literally sell their daughters to men in order to survive? Why is there no hesitation in driving a car into the river with your children strapped in the seat?

From the beginning of Jesus' ministry, He said the greatest command of all is to *love* the Father with our whole heart, body, and soul. Second, we are commanded to love ourselves. Then, third, we are to love the neighbor.

But, how are we to learn about love?

It is all about you—the woman—the bond, the glue, that holds the family together.

What does the glue perform?

You, the *'em, the glue,* are to teach the younger women to Love their husbands and children. You—the *'em* are the only one who was given this command. This is why Satan came after the woman. This is why YOU are on the devil's hit list.

Yes, husbands can teach their children about love. But, if they were not taught by their mother, sisters, aunt, grandmothers, etc.

how to love themselves as a valuable creation by God, how can they in turn be a *loving* husband and father?

Love is the key. However, it is not the fickle love that the world teaches. The secular concept of love is binding, choking, and claiming alleged ownership of another human being, as some of the stories reveal. Thus, husbands kill entire families because they *belong* to him.

In complete contrast, the love that God said to teach is about freedom, *John 10:10*, and joy and peace, etc., wholeness, *Galatians 5: 22-23*. The ministers of love must follow this command. But, the ministers—the women—must first know it for themselves.

God created us for His purpose. He also prepared plans in advance for us to follow.

Ephesians 2:10.

Under the invisible demonic tutelage of abuse, emotionally injured men teach women to hate their own bodies through the ungodly acts of rape, molestation, etc. And, if the older woman has been abused and misused during her lifetime, then that is the same demonic spirit that she *unknowingly* passes on to her female daughter, as shown in the various chapters in *We Are One*.

God warned us that the devil was good at his job.

Nevertheless, by Faith, Christian believers have something that non-believers lack. We have an *in-built* I.P.S. system, which is the *Declared* Commands of God over our lives. For instance:

I.—the *unchanging* declaration of God in His Word, as to our *female* identity as God's *intended and designed* teachers to others how to love according to God's faithfulness and His love.

P.—the unchanging declaration of God that you—the woman—are *purposed* as the glue, the bond, that holds the family of God together through *Godly* love.

S. — the unchanging declared and written Word of God, Jesus, who came in the flesh to Declare the truth that He is the *source* of our strength.

This I.P.S. system is activated by Faith, i.e. *complete trust in the truthfulness of God, and reliance in Jesus for Salvation.* God said it. That settles it. And, when we are yoked together with Jesus, there is nothing the devil can do about it.

In 1996, while studying the woman in Proverbs 31, I drew a picture of a woman. The entire family, the husband, the children, the home, her job, and a teaching ministry all rest on her shoulders. This was about a year after my spiritual rebirth.

Although I scripturally knew very little yet, the Holy Spirit revealed my ordained purpose of encouraging women with His truth.

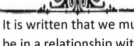

It is written that we must be in a relationship with the Son of God in order to produce fruit, i.e. accomplish our assigned missions.

Why does He do this? That when revelation comes to pass, we will believe in Him.

How serious is God about our assignment? The book of Job makes it clear that talking trust in God, and total belief in God, are two different things. This remains true today.

John 15: 4

Our heavenly Father is very serious about us fulfilling our commission. The following chapter makes it clear that God is unchanged.

The Body of Christ has a divine responsibility to fulfill our assignment.

Nonetheless, God tells us that He will put nothing on us that we cannot bear. Initially, I disagreed. However, some people tend to need more of God's hands-on intervention in order to understand and obey. Just saying.

Since I am here and alive today, I must and do acknowledge that Jesus was right.

Chapter 15 Study Guide

Women have been searching for the truth about their *rightful* place in the kingdom of Jesus Christ for centuries, such as the Queen of Sheba.

We Are One has revealed God's truth. This knowledge has been like a tree camouflaged by an Amazon-ish forest of *mis*interpretations and *re*interpretations, Matthew 15: 8-9.

God did not give the woman this assignment to fail. He Declared it. Thus it is so.

1. Do you believe that this divine assignment can change the world?

   a. If not, why?

      i. Discuss.

2. Do you believe that manmade doctrines can alter or nullify this assignment?

   a. Discuss.

3. *We Are One* illustrated that trials and tests come with this assignment.

   a. Are you ready?

      i. Discuss.

4. Are you already operating in this assignment?

    a.   If so, are you stumbling with the tests?

    b.   Have you activated your I.P.S. system?

It works.

Notes:

Chapter 16 – A Promise Bypasses Time

Yahovah said that before His True believers call, He will
answer; and while we are yet speaking, He will hear, Isaiah 65: 24

Y ou are trying to kill me. Get out."
The squish, squish, squish, of rubber soles on a
concrete floor announced the hasty exit of the nurses.
It was 3 a.m. A hazy light flickered across the bed from the crack
in the door.

Hospitalized a second time in two months with a
misdiagnosed disease, along with double Pneumonia, a 102.3
fever had ravaged my body. Nevertheless, a
feeling of Antarctic cold in my bones led to
uncontrollable convulsing of my body. The
tit, tat, tit, chattering of my teeth was the
only sound in the room. An earlier
conversation with my spiritual mentor,
regarding my complaints about the medical
negligence, surfaced.

Disbelief in the
authority of Jesus
can hinder healing.

Matthew 9: 23-25.

Only slightly conscious, I remembered
trying to explain a doctor's decision to withhold medicine as a
test to see how high my fever would climb. My mentor's
response to my complaint planted a seed in my mind. However,
the pain-numbing medicine knocked me out before her
suggestion could be implemented.

At 3 a.m., upon awaking from the drug induced fog, the
realization that I could die was foremost in my thoughts. I
remembered her comment.

"You are talking to the wrong person," she had said.

After the nurses left, I began to talk to the right Healer.

"Heavenly Father, in the name of your son Jesus, I thank you for a life of love and joy that I could never have imagined. Thank you for sending your Holy Spirit..."

Suddenly, in the midst of my prayer, an unusual heat started at the top of my left lung and moved slowly downward as I was speaking. It felt as though someone had poured a kettle of hot water inside my lung. Meanwhile, I kept talking while looking at my chest in amazement. When His Healing touch reached the bottom of my left lung, it stopped.

Side note. The convulsions ceased. It no longer felt as though the sub-freezing temperature of Alaska had taken up residence inside of my body.

"Wow," was my first thought. "Thank you. Wow. I must not be finished with my Godly assignment. Wow."

Amazement kept me awoke for a short period. The seven or eight blankets, that had failed to keep me warm, were thrown off. After again thanking God for His mercy, I turned over and went to sleep. At 6 a.m., the new shift of nurses found me sitting up on the side of the bed awake and cognizant. Later that morning, one nurse returned from the day before. God had called her back to witness the miracle.

"Oh my God," she cried out when she walked into the room. "I was weeping and praying so hard on the way home that I had to pull off to the side of the road. Look at you. You are a miracle."

"I know," I said with a huge grin and a hug.

The other nurses tried to claim that it was the medicine.

"How could that be when this hospital allowed a doctor to experiment on me through the denial of medication," I sharply retorted. "If not for God, I could have died."

They left the room.

This story would not be complete without the knowledge of a seemingly innocent act on my behalf that initiated this test. When the situation turned deadly, a strange uneasy sense about the reason arose in my mind. About a year later, the Holy Spirit revealed the answer.

It was supposed to be a minor surgery. Several blood tests had been completed. All were clean—no infections. During pre-op, as I lay surrounded by a multitude of others, their comments about their medical issues could be overheard. The amounts of medicine that their illnesses required on a daily basis were stunning.

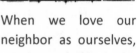

When we love our neighbor as ourselves, we have fulfilled the whole law of God.

Galatians 5:14.

My prayer—prior to my surgery—included thanking God for my own lack of physical problems. Yes, I know. Me and my mouth, even in thought. I did it again. However, this situation taught me a lesson that I will never forget. Until a person has walked in another's shoes, it is arrogant to claim that *I know how you feel.* I didn't.

Until that time, the total effect on a person's life and body due to whole body disability was lacking in my comprehension. More importantly to Jesus, my surroundings failed to prick my compassion meter—if you will—as His representative.

In approximately 24 hours after the operation, a blood infection raged through my body. The severity of it caused me to fall and reinjure the original surgery site in my knee. Over the next few months, the contamination coursed through my body and lodged in my lung. Of course, all and any contagion from a hospital procedure was denied.

Nevertheless, Jesus accepted my grateful prayer of repentance. Thereafter, the divine healing took place only in my left lung.

Medical history records over the years indicate that many people enter the hospital for minor surgery. Many do not return home. My assignment for Jesus was not completed. He forgave me for my failure to show Love and allowed me to return home to finish my assignment.

The men and women who protect this country in the military are called soldiers. Those who are called into the body and kingdom of Jesus Christ are soldiers, 2 *Timothy* 2:3-4. There is a single unchanging similarity between the two. Training and testing are required in both fields.

In the military, hopeful recruits must first attend a boot camp where they receive basic training through battling with mock enemies. The instructors put the enrollees through back-breaking physical drills as well as emotional challenges to help prepare them for upcoming battles against visible enemies.

Without such hard-core preparation, these future warriors that protect the United States would never have realized their inner strengths. All enrollees do not make it through boot camp.

Spiritual warfare is much the same. Training is required. The instructor, the Holy Spirit of God, is tough but fair. He knows that trials and tribulations build up the Christian's inner strength, 2 *Timothy* 2: 12. The specifics of His training manual come from the highest authority. They are included in my book: *Purposely Unchained.*

However, artillery is where the two military systems part company.

Military weapons are intended to kill. On the other hand, our spiritual arsenal is some of the strangest in existence. And, special training is required to use them for their intended purpose. They are specifically created for the mind of the believer. However, for me, the test of my faith is where an old adage came to pass. People often commented that the consequences of life are where the rubber meets the road due their own actions. In this case, the *rubber of my faith* met the road of my confessions.

It is one thing to say that we have faith in Jesus. But what does that really mean? Faith, i.e. Greek *Pistis,* means a total and complete trust in Jesus and total trust in the truthfulness of Yahovah's Word as to the identity of Jesus.

My profession of faith was tested. Despite my failure, there was no fear but acceptance in His Word that I was loved. Thus, I acknowledged my gratefulness for my life. He had allowed me to live a life of joy for the last 20 years, at that time. In lieu of my former life as an atheist, due to my childhood, a life serving Jesus as my Lord and Savior was a gift.

During my conversation with Jesus, I knew that my life was not in my hands, nor those of the physicians. My trust in His authority opened the door to the fulfillment of one of His Promises. My miraculous recovery illustrated several points. My service was not complete. My faith passed the test and became a witness to others that the promises of God are eternal. A lesson was learned about the importance of my—thus our—mission to the world. We, the women, are God's appointed ministers of Godly Love.

Jesus uses our faith to heal us, and as a witness to others.

Act 3:16.

Scriptures reveal that Jesus is very serious about our mission to the world. He told the first disciples that they would face adversity unlike anything they had ever known if they followed Him. In other words, Jesus did not trick them into following him and later tell them the truth, like mankind. He was upfront with them.

The word of God reveals that they really did not understand what Jesus meant. Numerous passages disclose that their minds, i.e. the way they thought about other people and themselves, would need to change. Specifically, Apostle Peter had to learn about forgiving others. In a nutshell, all of the disciples had to be instructed in how to truly love God the father first, love themselves second, and finally love the neighbor.

Time and again, as the disciples walked with Jesus for three years, Jesus exhibited these principles. Plainly, the growth of faith is a process. Curiosity about faith in situations that boggle the imagination led me to study Joseph.

Joseph was steadfast in his belief that God was directing his path through dreams, even though his brothers had betrayed him and tried to kill him. He ended up in Egypt as a slave. Eventually, he rose to extreme power and wealth and would save his family from the famine that God had shown him in the dreams.

But, how did this steadfast faith originate? And why did it take so long for me to trust in the dreams and revelations from God? The answer was in the Word of God.

Joseph had been taught by his father as a child about how God provides, teaches, and directs his people through dreams and actual meetings. In contrast, God also gave us knowledge as to the difference that upbringing has in our lives.

The life of Abraham highlights the opposite.

Unlike Joseph's parental guidance, Abraham's father believed in pagan gods. Nevertheless, Scripture reveals that God chose Abraham to be the progenitor of the spiritual seed of God.

This is my opinion. I believe Yahovah, our heavenly Father and God, chose Abraham, and *me*, and others, to show His people that no matter what our background involves, no matter the trials and lifestyles, He loves us. And, we *all* are able to change under His tutorship.

The difference in their upbringing is even more varied in their walks of faith.

Joseph maintained his faith from childhood to death. Abraham was called to purpose when he was 75. However, it took another 30 plus years for Abraham to arrive at a level of faith that still today astounds the imagination. He lifted the knife to slay his son. But, the reader of the word of God gets a preview that his faith had grown.

In Genesis 22, verse five, Abraham tells the servants to stay put and that he and his son will return. He and his son continue to the selected place of sacrifice. In verse 10, Abraham lifts the knife to kill his son. God tells him to stop and provides him with a ram in the bush.

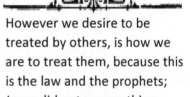

However we desire to be treated by others, is how we are to treat them, because this is the law and the prophets; Jesus did not say anything about whether their behavior is good, bad, or ugly.

Matthew 7: 12

In other words, Abraham made a declaration of faith *before* God provided the ram. Abraham's faith had grown to such a level that he knew that regardless of what would happen at the place of sacrifice, he would yet have a son because God had promised. God kept His Word.

This is my opinion. I believe Yahovah, our heavenly Father and God, chose Abraham, and *me*, and others like us, to show the world that no matter what our background involves, no matter the trials and lifestyles, He loves us. And, we *all* are able to change under His tutorship.

God never tells us to do what is impossible. The biblical stories prove that faith is essential. And, God alone knows when we are ready for the mission to which we are appointed, as the varied stories in *We Are One* demonstrate. God kept His Word.

Tests of our faith are unavoidable. My faith in Jesus grew stronger with each one.

God allowed me to taste true disability. Help was needed for even the basics of living: going to the restroom, getting into and out of bed, washing my body, etc. It was a humbling experience.

God gets all the glory for my new life. The steps that He used to change me from an atheist to an ambassador for His Son Jesus, inclusive of growth and falls, are recorded in both of my books, *Mine, an Everlasting Promise of Love...,* and *Purposely Unchained.* In particular, His divine orchestrated instructions, that are included in *Purposely Unchained,* took the level of my faith to what I call a *Joseph* faith. If not for that training, I would not have been able to face the possibility of death without fear.

God's advice works. Thus, my faith response to the prospect of death was not a surprise. It was a "shades of Abraham faith" moment.

The knowledge and truth of my identity, my purpose, and the source of my strength who is Jesus, was the *truth belt* that kept all the other pieces of armor locked in place when faced with the possibility of death. It kept fear at bay.

How serious is Jesus about the strength of our faith? He turned Apostle Peter over to the devil to let Peter know that his mindset of self-preservation was not appropriate for a representative of Jesus. Ananias and his wife died because they pretended to have faith. King Saul lost his kingdom because he stopped obeying the commandments of Yahovah. There are too many instances to recount.

The bottom line is that the body of Christ has a pre-ordained purpose. In particular, the women of God have an assignment that will change the world.

If I were asked to give a synopsis of my commission, it would be that I am to remind the women of God that we are God's purposed ministers to teach the world His love. You, we, the women, are God's *ministers of love* who are to teach others how to love in a Godly manner.

Now don't get this twisted. Jesus is not talking about love as the world identifies it. Nor are we to love the *actions* of people who are defying the commandments of Jesus. We are to Love the people, as a whole, as the creation of the one and only true and living God, who made us all in His image and likeness. Period.

God will handle their disobedience.

This lesson of *Love* for others forever changed my view of death and how Jesus views people that He alone died to save. Thus, as His representative, it is our job to spiritually love them the same. He did not say based on their behavior or faith. He said love them.

It is His command.

Chapter 16 Study Guide

Faith, Prayer, and Love, are the key to a relationship with Jesus. Faith and Love are like two sides of a coin. Prayer is the long-distance cord that connects to God. Faith in His love will make you do strange things. Faith led the woman with the issue of blood to defy tradition and go out in public to touch the hem of Jesus' garment. Faith led Queen Esther to defy tradition, which could have led to her death. To save her daughter, Faith led a woman to declare that even the crumbs off of the master's table were sufficient. Jesus called her faith Great faith.

Faith, i.e. total trust in the truthful of God, and reliance upon Jesus for salvation, still works as this story reveals. More so, even when faced with death. More so, God uses our *show* of faith to show others His omnipotence and faithfulness of love.

1.   What strange thing has faith led you to do, and when you looked back, you knew it was God that brought you through.
2.
a.   Did you tell others?

    i.   If not, why not?

Notes:

Conclusion: The Woman – No Longer the Missing Link

History reveals that the world has searched for answers to the world's problems of hate, bigotry, rape, murder, etc. Prisons, mental institutions, and the grave, testify to the failure by mankind to control the problem. Numerous books have been written on the reasons. Yet, the solution is right in front of them.

False religion added to the problem by erroneously teaching that women have little value, if any. Up to and until today, many women have accepted this erroneous concept to be true because the importance and *essential need* of our preordained purpose has been concealed.

The chapters of *We Are One* bring out a stunning Eternal truth. Better yet, it will forever change your life.

YOU, the WOMAN, have always been the key to changing the world.

Satan knows this truth, thus his continuous attacks on women. You, the Woman, are indispensable in God's plan. You, the Woman - are the *Missing Link* that was designated *by God* in the beginning to bring His desires to fruition on earth.

Through the influence of Satan—starting with Eve in the Garden of Eden—many women have come to accept God's wondrous creation of the female as a second-hand, bargain basement, mistake.

187

God does not make errors.

The atrocious, demonic acts perpetrated against especially females, from childhood to adulthood, serve a single goal. They are demonic acts in the attempt to deflect us from operating in our assigned role for God. More so, the stories of the women in *We Are One* clearly demonstrate that Satan is not prejudiced.

The devil's goal is to kill, steal, and destroy, the people of God regardless of race, religion, or origin. Through the various stories in *We Are One,* this truth becomes obvious.

The Word of God makes it clear to believers about this eternal enemy. And, as the stories of women in *We Are One* reveal, that seed is most vulnerable in children. Thus, the devil's continuous attack on children, especially females.

The result is that especially women are caught up in a trap of deception that leaves many unaware of their godly purpose. The devil knew that if he could bring enough hurt, pain, and anger, into the woman's life, her method of operation in the world would change. *We Are One* reveals the consequences.

Nevertheless, God is in control.

God presented a question to the prophet in Amos 3: 3. *How can two walk together except they agree?* What the English translation left out was that in order to agree, they must first meet. For the true followers of Jesus, we must first meet Him, and then agree to follow His steps.

False religion has also duped women into accepting the ungodly concept that the only place for women in the kingdom of Jesus Christ is as undeserving and weak followers of men. The world today, secular and Christian, prove the devastating consequences of this action because the woman is not in her designated place of purpose as designed by God.

The first woman was given a specific appointment. It applies to every female. *We Are One* also reveals that God gave the woman biblical instructions in how to succeed in her part of this essential task that was declared by God.

The fulfilling of our assignment will change the world per God's specifications. Nonetheless, through subterfuge and reinterpretation of the Word of God, even in the world of religion, a woman's divine job has been kept a secret.

Satan knew the lack of knowledge of our ordained directive would have disastrous consequences, as revealed by a few of the stories in the various chapters of *We Are One*.

Every woman's journey in this book, and her ability to handle the trials of her life, can be traced back to what she *heard* as a child. If they were true words about God, and His amazing love for His creation, persecution could not shake her faith. On the other hand, those who heard negative concepts about God and their place in the world were tested to the point of destruction.

In a few cases, the devil succeeded in his goal to steal, kill, and destroy. *We Are One* illustrates that death is not always physical.

Ladies, your faith in Jesus, and your trust in the truthfulness of God's Word, was and is the target that the devil is truly after. This battle between good and evil is a no-holds-barred fight. Fast forwarding to the 21st century, God's plans are unchanged and neither have Satan's.

The devil does not rent a billboard alongside Highway 101 to advertise his moves. He doesn't even have a web page. He is far more subtle. *We Are One* discloses his methods.

Our Promised protection is through *true* knowledge of *Thus Said the Lord*.

It is the author's prayer and hope that the Word of God, along with these true stories, will inspire and encourage women to stand up and step into their ordained assignment, and tell the devil, *No More*.

It is time to activate your I.P.S. system.

Personal Story Directory

CPSIA information can be obtained
at www.ICGtesting.com
Printed in the USA
BVHW032258170519
548584BV00001B/67/P